# WALKING WITH ENOCH

*IT'S YOUR TURN!*

## STUDY GUIDE

# WALKING WITH ENOCH

*It's Your Turn!*

## STUDY GUIDE

Dr. Kevin L. Zadai

© Copyright 2023 Kevin L. Zadai. All rights reserved. This book is protected by the copyright laws of the United States of America. This book may not be copied or reprinted for commercial gain or profit. The use of short quotations or the copying of an occasional page for personal or group study is permitted and encouraged. Permission will be granted upon request. Unless otherwise indicated, Scripture quotations are taken from the New King James Version. Copyright © 1982 by Thomas Nelson, Inc. Used by permission. All rights reserved. All Scripture quotations marked (KJV) are taken from the King James Version. Public Domain. Scripture quotations marked (NLT) are taken from the Holy Bible, New Living Translation, copyright ©1996, 2004, 2015 by Tyndale House Foundation. Used by permission of Tyndale House Publishers, a Division of Tyndale House Ministries, Carol Stream, Illinois 60188. All rights reserved. Scripture quotations marked (AMP) are taken from the Amplified Bible, Copyright © 1954, 1958, 1962, 1964, 1965, 1987 by The Lockman Foundation. Used by permission. www.Lockman.org. Scripture quotations marked "NASB" are taken from the New American Standard Bible®, Copyright © 1960, 1962, 1963, 1968, 1971, 1972, 1973, 1975, 1977, 1995 by The Lockman Foundation. Used by permission. www.Lockman.org. Scripture quotations taken from the Amplified® Bible (AMPC), Copyright © 1954, 1958, 1962, 1964, 1965, 1987 by The Lockman Foundation. Used by permission. lockman.org. Scripture quotations marked (TPT) are from The Passion Translation®. Copyright © 2017, 2018 by Passion & Fire Ministries, Inc. Used by permission. All rights reserved. www.thePassionTranslation.com. Scripture quotations marked "ESV" are from the ESV Bible® (The Holy Bible, English Standard Version®), copyright © 2001 by Crossway Bibles, a publishing ministry of Good News Publishers. Used by permission. All rights reserved. http://www.crossway.org. Scripture quotations marked "MSG" or "The Message" are taken from The Message. Copyright 1993, 1994, 1995, 1996, 2000, 2001, 2002. Used by permission of NavPress Publishing Group. http://www.navpress.com/. The Living Bible copyright © 1971 by Tyndale House Foundation. Used by permission of Tyndale House Publishers Inc., Carol Stream, Illinois 60188. All rights reserved. The Living Bible, TLB, and the The Living Bible logo are registered trademarks of Tyndale House Publishers.

Please note that Warrior Notes publishing style capitalizes certain pronouns in Scripture that refer to the Father, Son, and Holy Spirit, which may differ from some publishers' styles. Take note that the name "satan" and related names are not capitalized. We choose not to acknowledge him, even to the point of violating accepted grammatical rules. The author and Warrior Notes have made an intentional decision to italicize many Scriptures in block quotes. This is our own emphasis, not the publisher's.

Warrior Notes Publishing
P O Box 1288
Destrehan, LA 70047

Cover design: Virtually Possible Designs

For more information about our school, go to www.warriornotesschool.com. Reach us on the internet: www.Kevinzadai.com

ISBN 13 TP: 978-1-6631-0099-3

# Dedication

I dedicate this book to the Lord Jesus Christ. When I died during surgery and met with Jesus on the other side, He insisted that I return to life on the earth and that I help people with their destinies. Because of Jesus' love and concern for people, the Lord has actually chosen to send a person back from death to help everyone who will receive that help so that his or her destiny and purpose is secure in Him. I want You, Lord, to know that when You come to take me to be with You someday, it is my sincere hope that people remember not me, but the revelation of Jesus Christ that You have revealed through me. I want others to know that I am merely being obedient to Your Heavenly calling and mission, which is to reveal Your plan for the fulfillment of the divine destiny for each of God's children.

# Acknowledgements

In addition to sharing my story with everyone through the book *Heavenly Visitation: A Guide to the Supernatural,* God has commissioned me to write over sixty books and study guides. Most recently, the Lord gave me the commission to produce this study guide, *Walking With Enoch.* This study guide addresses some of the revelations concerning the areas that Jesus reviewed and revealed to me through the Word of God and by the Spirit of God during several visitations. I want to thank everyone who has encouraged me, assisted me, and prayed for me during the writing of this work. Special thanks to my wonderful wife, Kathi, for her love and dedication to the Lord and me. Thank you to a great staff for the wonderful job editing this book. Special thanks as well to all my friends who know about *Walking With Enoch* and how to operate in this for the next move of God's Spirit!

# Contents

Introduction..................................................................................................1

Chapter 1 Enoch Pleases God ...................................................................3

Chapter 2 The Lineages, Their Names, and Prophesies.............................13

Chapter 3 The Days of Noah......................................................................25

Chapter 4 God is Grieved with Mankind...................................................35

Chapter 5 The Powers of the Coming Age................................................47

Chapter 6 God Rewards the Diligent.........................................................59

Chapter 7 God's Battle Strategies..............................................................85

Chapter 8 The Intensity of Serving God....................................................105

Chapter 9 The Bold and Righteous Ones Persevere..................................127

Chapter 10 Tenacity is in You....................................................................149

# Introduction

Our love for God and relationship with Him are the central, most important factors in executing His plans and purposes. Enoch was regarded as one that held such high honor towards God, and it pleased Him. He pursued God with a tenacity and faith that compelled God to translate him often until one day when God plucked him out of the earth to be with him forever. We can learn from the character traits of Enoch and how he withstood the tests of the culture of the day and remained faithful to His Lord. He honored the Lord despite the calamities around him. Humanity was unfaithful, and evil abounded, but Enoch's steadfast love for God remained true. He was one that remained Godly from the lineage of Adam and kept a standard in his generation and for generations to come. Through this extensive teaching, you will be fully equipped with all that you need to uphold God's righteousness and purity on the earth and live to proclaim the Gospel and fulfill your assignment!

Blessings,
Dr. Kevin L. Zadai

# CHAPTER ONE

# Enoch Pleases God

*So whether we are here in this body or away from this body, our goal is to please him.*
—*2 Corinthians 5:9 NLT*

**DISCUSSION:**

Enoch was known as one of the Old Testament prophets from whom we can glean knowledge. He walked closely with God and was taken up to be with the Lord because he pleased God so much. He is first mentioned in Genesis and is part of Adam's lineage. We see him being talked about extensively through the book of Hebrews. He is the seventh generation of Adam and came from Seth's line. The sin of Cain and the murder of his brother Abel were where the bloodlines begin to divert.

Everything originated from the line of Adam. His lineage was supposed to live forever. They were never supposed to die. The sons of God were the sons of Adam. *'Āḏām*[1] in Hebrew is the word for *man*, and this eternal being was never supposed to

---

[1] "H120 - 'āḏām - Strong's Hebrew Lexicon (kjv)." Blue Letter Bible. Accessed 20 Jan, 2023. https://www.blueletterbible.org/lexicon/h120/kjv/wlc/0-1/

sin, get sick, or die. They were still pure to a certain degree, which is why it took Adam 930 years to die.

Even though Adam and Eve were taken out of the garden, they still had conversations with God. We see in Scripture where God came to Cain and coached him when he had not done the proper procedures for the sacrifice (Genesis 4:1-7). It appears that God was still visiting mankind even after the fall. For them not to live physically eternally, they could not eat from the tree of life anymore. They were cut off physically and spiritually, but it didn't happen immediately. If you look at the lineages, life expectancy began to deteriorate, and they lived for shorter periods.

Adam lived for 930 years, and Methuselah died at 969 years old. He's the oldest recorded in the lineage. As you get into the line to Abraham, their life expectancy went down to 200 years, then it reduced to 120 years, and now mankind lives to be about 70-80 years on average. The people were also cut off spiritually, physically, and in their souls. God still visited with them for a while, but their physical part began to deteriorate, and their spiritual position weakened. The sons of God were the line of Adam. Once you get into Cain's family line, it goes downhill quickly because of the curse God put on him.

God said the serpent's seed and the woman's seed would be in warfare, and there would be enmity between the serpent's and woman's seed. When looking at the curse and how Cain was accursed and marked, you can see how the serpent's seed got into his bloodline. You have fallen man, and then Adam's other sons, who continued to walk with God, such as Noah's sons, Shem, Ham, and Japheth, whom God kept clean. Then on the other side, there were people related to Cain in his curse. He married one of Adam's daughters and had many children, including Enoch. However, Enoch was Godly.

- ❖ **Genesis 5:18-19 AMPC:**

When Jared was 162 years old, Enoch was born. Jared lived after the birth of Enoch 800 years and had other sons and daughters.

- Jared was one of the sons in that line.
- He lived for 800 years after the birth of Enoch.
- They were still walking with God in some respects.
- The Godly line of Adam was in their biology, and it took a long time for them to die.
- Sin hadn't worked through the physical, spiritual, and soulical realms.

- ❖ **Genesis 5:21-24 AMPC:**

When Enoch was 65 years old, Methuselah was born. Enoch walked [in habitual fellowship] with God after the birth of Methuselah 300 years and had other sons and daughters. So all the days of Enoch were 365 years. And Enoch walked [in habitual fellowship] with God; and he was not, for God took him [home with Him].

- When Enoch was 65 years old, he walked with God.
- He walked with God for 300 years.
- As soon as Methuselah was born, Enoch walked with God.
- Enoch was taken at 365 years old.

- It is symbolic because there are 365 days a year, and Enoch walked with God every day after that.
- It's a parallel for us to walk with God every day, 365 days a year.
- In verse 22, it says, "Enoch walked in habitual fellowship with God, after the birth of Methuselah 300 years and had other sons and daughters." Enoch had other sons and daughters, but only certain individuals were mentioned.
- The idea here is to see what happened in the time of Noah.
- There is a science to figuring out how many people would be on the earth during the flood based on living for hundreds of years and having children. It would have been millions of people.
- The same is true for animals. Studies prove this and have determined how many animals and of what type were on the earth then.
- Enoch bore Methuselah. There are secret messages hidden about their name. Many details can be revealed if you look up their family name meaning and lineage.

**At what age did Enoch begin to walk with God?**

_____
_____
_____
_____

**What do you think habitual fellowship looks like?**

_____

_____

_____

_____

## GOD TAKES ENOCH

**DISCUSSION:**

Genesis is a prophetic book written by Moses on the mountain of God. Scripture says that he received the law from the angels. We know that he was dictating a document called Genesis because he had yet to be born during the writing of Genesis. 1 Chronicles 1:3 talks about Enoch, Methuselah, and Lamech and verifies the genealogies found in Genesis.

Luke 3:37 says, "The son of Methuselah, the son of Enoch, the son of Jared, the son of Mahalalel, the son of Cainan." Here is another Scripture in the New Testament that verifies these genealogies in the Old Testament. We have several references that back up what's written in Genesis.

The book of Hebrews reveals a great deal about Enoch and unfolds how he thinks and the mindset of the day. We will look at a few different translations of Hebrews 11:5-6 to get a deeper understanding of the verse and its contextual meaning.

## ❖ Hebrews 11:5-6 TPT :

Faith translated Enoch from this life and he was taken up into heaven! He never had to experience death; he just disappeared from this world because God promoted him. For before he was translated to the heavenly realm his life had become a pleasure to God. And without faith living within us it would be impossible to please God. For we come to God in faith knowing that he is real and that he rewards the faith of those who passionately seek him.

- Enoch was caught up and transferred into Heaven.
- These verses here are prophetic for the end-time events.
- Enoch was a prophet; sometimes, God used prophets with their whole life as prophetic statements.
- It includes the genealogies, dates, times, and the number of years they lived. Their whole lives are prophetic.

**What was it that translated Enoch to Heaven?**

_____
_____
_____
_____

**For what purpose does God consider someone to be a prophet?**

_____
_____
_____
_____

❖ **<u>Hebrews 11:5-6 MSG:</u>**

By an act of faith, Enoch skipped death completely. "They looked all over and couldn't find him because God had taken him." We know on the basis of reliable testimony that before he was taken, "he pleased God." It's impossible to please God apart from faith. And why? Because anyone who wants to approach God must believe both that he exists *and* that he cares enough to respond to those who seek him.

❖ **<u>Hebrews 11:5-6 TLB:</u>**

Enoch trusted God too, and that is why God took him away to Heaven without dying; suddenly, he was gone because God took him. Before this happened, God had said how pleased he was with Enoch. You can never please God without faith, without depending on him. Anyone who wants to come to God must believe that there is a God and that he rewards those who sincerely look for him.

- It says, "Enoch trusted God," and that is why God took him.
- The word faith is not used here in this translation. The word *trust* is used, which is more accurate because the Hebrew word for faith is the word trust.
- Trust is the reason God took Enoch away without him having to die.
- Before this happened, God said *He was pleased with Enoch.*
- You can never please God without faith or depending upon Him.

**What is the key to coming to God in this verse?**

_____
_____
_____
_____

**How does God respond to those who look for Him?**

_____
_____
_____
_____

- ❖ **Jude 1:14 AMPC:**

    It was of these people, moreover, that Enoch in the seventh [generation] from Adam prophesied when he said, Behold, the Lord comes with His myriads of holy ones (ten thousands of His saints).

    - Jude is referring to Enoch as being a prophet who came from Adam.
    - The book of Enoch, which is not part of the holy canon (the 66 books of the Bible), is part of the pseudepigrapha, which includes additional books mentioned in the Bible. One of which is the book of Jasher.
    - The pseudepigrapha is a compilation of additional writings not included in the Holy Canon. I mainly stay with the 66 books in the Bible, but I also read the other books for informational purposes.
    - Here, Jude quotes verbatim the first book of Enoch: the first revelation of Enoch.

- Jude read the book of Enoch even though it didn't make it into the Bible.
- The book of Enoch was accepted at one time and was voted out.
- There were questionable things in Enoch's book that did not follow suit with what we know as being standard in the Bible previously.
- For books to be considered in the Holy Canon, there are specific criteria they have to follow.
- When they considered the book of James to be included in the Holy Canon, it didn't make it in the first couple of times; it was later accepted.
- For books to be considered or accepted, it helps if they refer to another person and other books in the Bible.
- That's why Enoch was considered because Jude is quoting him.
- Enoch was prophesied on the earth at the time, as was Noah.
- We have certain prophets that came right before the flood.
- Noah was a preacher of righteousness.

**What is Enoch prophesying about in Jude 1:14?**

_____
_____
_____
_____

# CHAPTER TWO

# The Lineage, Their Names and Prophecies

*This is the book of the generations of Adam. In the day that God created man, in the likeness of God made he him;*
—*Genesis 5:1 KJV*

**DISCUSSION:**

From the time of Adam and Eve to the Days of Noah and the flood were a couple of thousand years. People had procreated then, and the earth became heavily populated. God had a purpose in mind, and we see that transpire in the prophetic book of Genesis as the genealogies are presented. The fallen world was present, and humanity fell into various classifications, one of which was the sons of God. They are not to be confused with angels as sons, and the book of Hebrews clears up this misconception (Hebrews 1:5). Angels were beings sent to assist God and mankind in God's purposes on earth. In the original text, there are different words used for angels. When they could have used the word for angel, they did not; they referred to them as sons of God.

There were specific traits Enoch had that helped him accomplish what he did. He pleased God so much, yet he didn't have the tools we have today or the new covenant. It was still the timeframe of the Old Testament. The book of Enoch talks about three visions Enoch had. These are not included in the Holy Canon. One account was a vision before and another after the flood. The last one is the vision of the end of days, which shows the Lord coming back and reveals how in tune Enoch was.

Methuselah is a key component to what's going on because his name means *death shall bring* or *send forth*. It's odd to have a name that means *his death shall bring*. That's the actual meaning of Methuselah. Enoch had a son named Methuselah, and the year that Methuselah was born, it says that Enoch began to walk with God. That became the reference point in this physical realm and the catalyst that initiated the timeline. God's mercy and plan are sometimes not known by man. Then, People like Samson are born to fulfill a specific purpose. Events occur that push forward what God is trying to do. We see this in the lives of Samuel and Moses when they were born. There were profound things that occurred and prophecies that came before they were born. The angel visited Samson's mother and then his father. The visitation was about Samuel being set apart and Moses. You see how God preserved his life.

God works within genealogies and bloodlines. They are part of a timeline and reference point. When Jesus was born, even the astrologers, who were magicians, came, but they came because of His star, not because of Him.

The shepherds came, and the angels announced His birth; the kings came because of the star and for a different intention, but it ended up being for the right reason. The initiation of the Lord being on the Earth began a sequence of events. Until that point, it was all prophesied.

When Enoch was born, something began, and it was the same for Methuselah when he was born. Some people interpret *Methuselah* to mean *his death shall bring*. Methuselah's father, Enoch, prophesied the coming flood. He was told that his son would live until the flood. That was part of the prophecy if you research it. The judgment of the flood would be withheld, but as soon as Methuselah died, the flood came forth. Enoch was going around to the cities, prophesying the flood.

People were interbreeding, so they didn't have redemption or repentance. They weren't given the gift of repentance. These particular people were not fully human. They were part of another bloodline connected to the serpent and his seed. God said the serpent's seed would get into humankind and affect the woman's seed.

The Messiah was to come through the proper lineage of the woman's seed. The different genealogies in the Bible reveal that there was no reptilian blood. No serpent seed had gotten in. The people were not half-breeds or hybrids. All the people in the genealogies show that Jesus was a pure human being and a spotless lamb. He was of pure human stock and came through the womb of Mary by the Holy Spirit, and *his death shall bring*. It is documented that when Methuselah died, it was the year the flood came. Methuselah was a living prophecy. He lived for 969 years.

It's essential to see that God was initiating His timeline. It wasn't man's timeline but God's who was creating things. That's what we need to know about God and why

Enoch was doing what he was doing. It was part of a bigger plan. It seems obscure until God has a deliverer or a prophet in the womb. When that prophet and deliverer comes forth, it begins an initiation and becomes a domino effect. Something was initiated as soon as Jesus was on the ground in a manger. From that point on, a sequence of events is prophesied. Methuselah died, and the flood came. The whole lineage beginning in Genesis 5, talks about each of the sons that were begotten. Adam was the first man; his name means *man*, and Adam bore Seth.

## NAMES AND THEIR MEANINGS

- **Genesis 5:3 AMP:**
  When Adam had lived a hundred and thirty years, he became the father of *a son* in his own likeness, according to his image, and named him Seth.

- **Genesis 5:6 AMP:**
  When Seth was a hundred and five years old, he became the father of Enosh.

- **Genesis 4:25-26:**
  And Adam knew his wife again, and she bore a son and named him Seth, "For God has appointed another seed for me instead of Abel, whom Cain killed." And as for Seth, to him also a son was born; and he named him Enosh. Then *men* began to call on the name of the LORD.

- Seth[2], which is *šēṯ* in Hebrew, at its root means *appointed.* Seth then had a son named Enosh.

- Enosh[3] is *'ĕnôš in Hebrew* and means *mortal, frail, or miserable.*

- There is significance to people's names and why they have them.

- Their names are prophetic and have hidden messages within them.

- The primitive root word for Enosh[4] or 'ānaš in Hebrew means *incurable* due to incurable diseases. His name also means "*wound, grief, woe, sickness,*" and possibly "*wickedness.*"

- In Genesis 4:26, the King James and New King James Version say that in the days of Enosh, "men began to call upon the name of the Lord."

- It can also be translated as; *man began to defile the name of the Lord.*

- The word being used here is *ḥālal*[5]. It's missing from the text in the English translation.

- The translators did not translate the word because it didn't make sense to them. The word *ḥālal* means *profane.* Therefore, it should be read: *Men began to profanely call upon the name of the Lord.*

❖ **It's essential to do the word study in the original text to confirm the words to know the contextual meaning and why the writer would italicize words.**

---

[2] "H7896 - šîṯ - Strong's Hebrew Lexicon (kjv)." Blue Letter Bible. Accessed 20 Jan, 2023. https://www.blueletterbible.org/lexicon/h7896/kjv/wlc/0-1/
[3] "H582 - 'ĕnôš - Strong's Hebrew Lexicon (kjv)." Blue Letter Bible. Accessed 20 Jan, 2023. https://www.blueletterbible.org/lexicon/h582/kjv/wlc/0-1/
[4] "H605 - 'ānaš - Strong's Hebrew Lexicon (kjv)." Blue Letter Bible. Accessed 20 Jan, 2023. https://www.blueletterbible.org/lexicon/h605/kjv/wlc/0-1/
[5] "H2490 - ḥālal - Strong's Hebrew Lexicon (kjv)." Blue Letter Bible. Accessed 20 Jan, 2023. https://www.blueletterbible.org/lexicon/h2490/kjv/wlc/0-1/

- ❖ You want to know why they add some words and leave others out. They give the excuse for adding words to give direction or flavor to the text because Hebrew text can be choppy.

- ❖ The ancient Hebrew language is barely a language today. Now we have Aramaic, the language Jesus spoke, and what is used earlier in the New Testament.

**Why are names so significant, and why is God intentional with names?**
_____
_____
_____
_____

**Why should we research the meaning of words in the Bible and study the text in depth?**
_____
_____
_____
_____

- ❖ **<u>Genesis 5:9 AMP:</u>**
  When Enosh was ninety years old, he became the father of Kenan.

- The root word of the name Kenan or Cainan is *qînâ*[6], and it means *sorrow and dirge*. This is different than the name Canaan (Genesis 9:18).
- As Balaam looked down from the heights of Moab, he used a pun upon the name of the Kenites when he prophesied their destruction.
- In Scripture, we see that prophets will use a pun from that generation and play off that to emphasize a word or phrase.

❖ When reading, be careful to research the words to understand the deeper or hidden meanings.

❖ We don't always know why certain words are used or have a particular meaning, but if you study further, you'll see how it's verified in the text and why.

❖ **Genesis 5:12 AMP:**

When Kenan was seventy years old, he became the father of Mahalalel.

- *Mahalalel*[7] was the son of Kenan and the next in line.
- His name means *blessed, praise the name of God,* or *blessed God.*

❖ **Genesis 5:15 AMP:**

When Mahalalel was sixty-five years old, he became the father of Jared.

---

[6] "H7015 - qînâ - Strong's Hebrew Lexicon (kjv)." Blue Letter Bible. Accessed 2 Feb, 2023. https://www.blueletterbible.org/lexicon/h7015/kjv/wlc/0-1/

[7] "H4111 - mahălal'ēl - Strong's Hebrew Lexicon (kjv)." Blue Letter Bible. Accessed 21 Jan, 2023. https://www.blueletterbible.org/lexicon/h4111/kjv/wlc/0-1/

- *Jared*[8] was the son of Mahalalel.
- His name means *shall come down.*

### ❖ Genesis 5:18 AMP:

When Jared was a hundred sixty-two years old, he became the father of Enoch.

- Jared had *Enoch*[9] or *ḥănôḵ* in Hebrew; his name means *teaching, teacher, or to train* in the primitive root word.
- In the lineage, he is the first of four generations of preachers.
- Enoch is the earliest recorded prophecy.
- He prophesied the second coming of Christ.
- He was the seventh generation of Adam.

### ❖ Genesis 5:21 AMP:

When Enoch was sixty-five years old, he became the father of Methuselah.

- *Methuselah*[10], or *mᵊṯûšelaḥ* in Hebrew, is the son of Enoch, and his name means *"man of the dart"* and can also be translated to mean *"his death shall bring."*
- His name is linked to Cain.

---

[8] "H3381 - yārad - Strong's Hebrew Lexicon (kjv)." Blue Letter Bible. Accessed 21 Jan, 2023. https://www.blueletterbible.org/lexicon/h3381/kjv/wlc/0-1/

[9] "H2596 - ḥānak - Strong's Hebrew Lexicon (kjv)." Blue Letter Bible. Accessed 21 Jan, 2023. https://www.blueletterbible.org/lexicon/h2596/kjv/wlc/0-1/

[10] "H4968 - mᵊṯûšelaḥ - Strong's Hebrew Lexicon (kjv)." Blue Letter Bible. Accessed 24 Jan, 2023. https://www.blueletterbible.org/lexicon/h4968/kjv/wlc/0-1/

❖ **Genesis 5:25 AMP:**

When Methuselah was a hundred and eighty-seven years old, he became the father of Lamech.

- Lamech is linked to Cain's line, who inadvertently killed his son Tubal-Cain in a hunting accident.

❖ **Genesis 5:28-29 AMP:**

When Lamech was a hundred and eighty-two years old, he became the father of a son. He named him Noah, saying, "This one shall bring us rest *and* comfort from our work and from the [dreadful] toil of our hands because of the ground which the Lord cursed."

- Noah is the last in this genealogy.
- *Noah*[11] means to *"bring comfort, rest, or relief."*

❖ **Glossary of Names:**

| | |
|---|---|
| **Adam:** Man | **Seth:** Appointed |
| **Enosh:** Mortal | **Kenan:** Sorrow |
| **Mahalalel:** Blessed God | **Jared:** Shall come down |
| **Enoch:** Teaching coincided with the flood). | **Methuselah:** His death shall bring (His death |
| **Lamech:** Despairing | **Noah:** Rest and comfort |

---
[11] "H5146 - nōaḥ - Strong's Hebrew Lexicon (kjv)." Blue Letter Bible. Accessed 24 Jan, 2023. https://www.blueletterbible.org/lexicon/h5146/kjv/wlc/0-1/

❖ If you take the genealogy and read the meaning of the names from the Hebrew, it says,

*Man is appointed, mortal, sorrow,*
*but the blessed God shall come down teaching*
*that his death shall bring*
*the despairing rest.*

❖ It combines the meanings of all the names in one sentence. It is a prophecy about the timeline and Jesus Christ coming and bringing us into Sabbath rest. Each person has a purpose and meaning in God's plan.

**Write your thoughts about how the meaning and prophecy of the people's names reveal God's plan.**

_____
_____
_____
_____

❖ The year that Methuselah died, the flood came, and the next sequence began. The human race became extinguished. Your life is even more important. Think about how long you have lived, the genealogies, and the generations that came before you. God is in all of it. He is into families and bloodlines.

You can imagine the war occurring on the other side and how satan doesn't know what's happening. He's trying to figure it out through the positions of the stars. He's trying to push the timeline to make things happen sooner than later because he doesn't want God to have the advantage over him.

- Disembodied spirits came from the flood. Humans who lived were killed physically, but their spirits are still alive.
- They do not want to leave the area they were in before the flood.
- They have not been taken into judgment or torment yet.
- According to Peter, the angels that left are in chains right now.
- When Jesus addressed the legion of demons, they did not want Him to send them out of the area (Matthew 8:28-34).
- They didn't want Him to torment them before their time. Their time had not yet come.
- They were stationed where they were before the flood and didn't want Jesus to cast them out of the area.

❖ In the time we live, we see that the demon spirits have no clue what is going on, and satan is trying to figure out what God is doing.

❖ He tries to dominate people and create scenarios to push the timeline to get God to react.

**Discussion:**

Your name has a meaning. When put together, as the body of believers, we are part of God's plan. We're a fulfillment of prophecy and a secret code. All our names together mean something in this generation. We're here for a reason, and we should allow the Spirit of God to speak to us. He will show you the part you play and the revelation of your name in the time you are living.

**What's the meaning of your name, and how do you believe it is prophetic for today?**

_____
_____
_____
_____

**Why is satan so determined in these end times?**

_____
_____
_____
_____

# CHAPTER THREE

# The Days of Noah

*"When the Son of Man returns, it will be like it was in Noah's day.
In those days before the flood, the people were enjoying banquets and parties and weddings right up to the time Noah entered his boat. People didn't realize what was going to happen until the flood came and swept them all away.
That is the way it will be when the Son of Man comes.*
—Matthew 24:37-39 NLT

**DISCUSSION:**

Jesus said that when He returns, it will be just like it was in the days of Noah. To understand and grasp what Jesus meant, we must look at what it was like in the Days of Noah. The first of four generations of preachers that preached was Enoch. Several individuals were prophesying and warning of the impending judgment coming upon the earth. Enoch's son, Methuselah, died that year, and it was prophesied that when he died, the flood would come. Enoch informed the people that within that year, the flood would come. There's a lot of controversy about Genesis 6 concerning this and the fallen angels, the Nephilim. What people were experiencing was intense. There's a lot happening today regarding blood, genes, DNA, and what's happening on the earth. We're discovering that certain diseases were being manufactured as warfare against countries. We see how they've been engineered and that messenger RNA is involved in implementing disease to weaken our DNA and immune system.

We now know we can splice the seed of an animal and make hybrids. That technology is available, and it's in the wrong hands. It's only a matter of time before we see mutations occurring. I believe that these things are already on the earth. Programs are in place to develop super soldiers, where they can alter one's DNA to make a superhuman. It's a form of hybridizing. They can alter your DNA with animals to bring out certain traits to alter your skin and your hair. Certain animals have traits that would favor a person if they wanted to be stronger or take on superhuman qualities. Animals have DNA that you can use to strengthen a particular area, such as your skin or muscles. The only thing is that God made man in His image. That's the perfect plan and blueprint.

If you were to compare someone's blueprint today and their DNA was altered, you would have to compare that with what God has announced is a human being. If it went past a certain point, then God would not call them human anymore, and then they wouldn't be redeemable because His whole idea was to bring back the original man. Mankind fell, then Jesus came as a pure human being, a spotless lamb.

The point is being *perfect in their generation, in their bloodline.* "Noah was a just man, perfect in his generations," the Bible says, and he was kept (Genesis 6:9). Only eight people were perfect. It's the idea of the perfect, spotless Lamb. In the Old Testament, when there was a spot or mark found on a lamb, it was considered a genetic defect.

They would not accept that lamb as a perfect sacrifice when you brought your animals to be sacrificed at the temple; they would reject it. It had to be a spotless lamb, free from defects.

### ❖ Genesis 6:1-3 AMPC:

When men began to multiply on the face of the land and daughters were born to them, The sons of God saw that the daughters of men were fair, and they took wives of all they desired and chose. Then the Lord said, My Spirit shall not forever dwell and strive with man, for he also is flesh; but his days shall yet be 120 years.

- Moses, the author of Genesis, wrote down what God dictated to him from the mountain.
- If you recall, we discussed what happened in chapter 5 with the genealogies, and their downfall was not good. Men were profanely calling on the name of the Lord.
- In Genesis chapter 6, "men began to multiply on the face of the earth, and daughters were born to them."
- The daughters represented the womb. That's the seed of the woman.
- The serpent's seed is also involved because God cursed man, the serpent, and the earth.
- Mankind began to multiply but had fallen through the line of Cain.
- Therefore, there were fewer remaining from Adam's pure stock.
- Not many from his lineage were walking with God.

- From Adam came his sons. Cain's line was cursed, and the entirety of Adam's bloodline began to degrade with each generation.
- Verse two says, "the sons of God saw the daughters of men." It refers to the common man and the daughters born to these men on the land.
- Moses used the words "*Benei Elohim,*" meaning *the sons of God.* Some scholars believe he was talking about angels, but Moses would've used a different word for that.
- There were two types of people living on the earth; those continuing the line of Adam and those degrading it more quickly.
- It reached a point where the sons of God were not allowed to take the daughters of men for their wives anymore because it was deteriorating the people.
- You wouldn't want your lineage breeding with these lines.

❖ **I believe the serpent's seed got into the people through Cain. We don't know exactly how that happened. Cain's wife was the daughter of Adam, but why does it say in the text, "they took wives of all they desired and chose."? If we take the text literally, it means they were being taken forcefully.**

❖ **You can't have the pure and Godly line interbreeding with those whose bloodlines were tainted. God tried to preserve the lineage to a certain degree, but it was a losing battle because of man's will.**

❖ **The Lord said, "My spirit will not forever dwell and strive with man for he is also flesh, but his days shall be 120 years." He could have also meant that there were 120 years left or that He would not allow mankind to live past a certain point because of interbreeding.**

**What are your thoughts concerning how the pure and Godly stock could interbreed with the people that were tainted?**
_____
_____
_____
_____

**Through whom did fallen man come into the lineages?**
_____
_____
_____
_____

**What does God finally do about mankind?**
_____
_____
_____
_____

❖ **<u>Genesis 6:4 AMPC:</u>**

There were giants on the earth in those days–and also afterward–when the sons of God lived with the daughters of men, and they bore children to them. These were the mighty men who were of old, men of renown.

- The word used for giant doesn't necessarily mean that they were larger physically.
- They were mighty ones, which means they had particular superhuman strengths and abilities.
- They had physical mutations.
- Their bodies were enhanced, and they were supernatural as well.
- They were hybrids; therefore, some of them had six fingers and six toes. They also had other defects.
- If you look up the word *"fallen"* in the Strong's Concordance, it's *nāp̄al*[12]. The plural word of *nāp̄al* is *Nephilim*[13]. The *im* is what makes it plural to mean *"fallen ones."*
- Genesis 6:4 reads: "The Nephilim were on the earth in those days."
- If you read the book of Enoch, you will see that the angels left their abode or their assignment (2 Peter 2:4). They are in chains now for what they did.
- The book of Enoch talks about how the fallen ones, or the Nephilim, taught the people how to sin.
- They came and corrupted and accelerated men to sin.

---

[12] "H5307 - nāp̄al - Strong's Hebrew Lexicon (kjv)." Blue Letter Bible. Accessed 28 Jan, 2023. https://www.blueletterbible.org/lexicon/h5307/kjv/wlc/0-1/

[13] "H5303 - nāp̄îl - Strong's Hebrew Lexicon (kjv)." Blue Letter Bible. Accessed 28 Jan, 2023. https://www.blueletterbible.org/lexicon/h5303/kjv/wlc/0-1/

- ❖ The Nephilim didn't go into the daughters of men; they were on the earth influencing human beings.

  - "The sons of God came into the daughters of men, and they bore children to them" (Genesis 6:4). These were the mighty men of old, men of renown.
  - It's talking about men, not the Nephilim or fallen angels.
  - The sons of man were going into the daughters of men.
  - The fallen angels left their abode and came down in those days on the earth.
  - They were on the earth, but it's as though they weren't supposed to be.
  - The fallen angels wrongly influenced God's sons and were forbidden to do so.
  - Ultimately hybrids came from this, not angels.
  - Angels are not given to marriage, nor are they married.
  - Jesus said that when you get to Heaven, you'll be like the angels, which are neither married nor given in marriage (Matthew 22:30).
  - Angels cannot marry and procreate based on what Jesus is saying.

- ❖ **When I was in Heaven, I had no clue or thought of marriage.**

- ❖ **Attraction toward the opposite sex and marriage took place on earth.**

**What were the men of renown doing?**

_____
_____
_____
_____


**What were the Nephilim doing?**

_____
_____
_____
_____


## HUMANITY TURNS TO EVIL

### DISCUSSION:

The children born from the sons of God were coming into the daughters of men. The sons of Adam, the pure stock of the line of Seth, came to where the women of Cain were and procreated with them. They were part of the serpent's seed that somehow got into the blood and genetics of human beings. After a while, the sons of God were not allowed to intermarry anymore with certain women. The children who were being born became mighty men or men of renown. There were gods, for example, like the Greek gods in mythology; they were half animal and half human. There were many different creatures on the earth pre-flood.

When archaeologists find bones and believe they discovered the origin of man and that we originated from apes, what they consider primitive man is essentially the interbreeding of man and animals. We didn't derive from that. Humanity was infiltrated from the pure stock and made to be half-human. When they find these skeletons and bones, they call it Cro-Magnom. The point is that these creatures or hybrids were being born. If you recall, Samson's parent's told him to stay with his people and not interbreed with other races. He did not obey (Judges 14:3).

### ❖ <u>**Genesis 6:5-6 AMPC:**</u>

The Lord saw that the wickedness of man was great in the earth, and that every imagination and intention of all human thinking was only evil continually. And the Lord regretted that He had made man on the earth, and He was grieved at heart.

- The Lord called it the wickedness of man.
- It wasn't the wickedness of angels; it was the wickedness of man because man is a central figure in all this.
- Enoch had to deal with wickedness in himself, but he was also dealing with the wickedness of everyone around him.
- There was great wickedness on the earth, and God had to limit how long men and women lived.
- Their imaginations, thoughts, and intentions were evil.
- It says their evil was continual. Can you imagine continual evil thoughts? That explains their continuous actions.
- Think about what you deal with today and multiply that by hundreds and hundreds of times.
- That's what they dealt with at the end before Noah's flood.

**How did evil infiltrate humanity?**

_____

_____

_____

_____

**Can you see how God had to bring the flood? Write about your overall thoughts concerning this chapter.**

_____

_____

_____

_____

# CHAPTER FOUR

# God is Grieved with Mankind

*And the LORD regretted that he had made man on the earth,*
*and it grieved him to his heart.*
—Genesis 6:6 ESV

**DISCUSSION:**

Moses wasn't alive during the time of the book of Genesis. He wrote it in his day on the mountaintop, as it was dictated word for word by the Lord and the angels. Moses had at least two forty-day sessions where he received dictation for the book. It was truly a supernatural occurrence.

"The Lord regretted that He had made man on the earth." It doesn't say that He regretted He made the earth. He regretted or repented that He made man on the earth. He was hurt over this mishap of man sinning and being exiled out of the garden due to all that happened from that point to Genesis 6. It was so bad. Can you imagine what it would have been like when Adam and Eve were kicked out of the garden?

It reached a point where God began to verbalize his displeasure of man's ways and determined to act. He was grieved in His heart for making man on earth. Romans 8:19-22 says, "all creation is groaning that the sons of God would be revealed." It's always been about mankind being sons of God. It's always been about man on earth, but creation fell, and now they're subject to the curse we caused. Animals and nature are groaning. Jesus fixed the issues of mankind and the fall through His death.

When Jesus came to the earth, He walked the right way. He was a perfect sacrifice and took care of the blood and genetic problem, dealing with it both spiritually and physically. He went back to Heaven. It's taken care of now, but we don't see everything in order because it has to play out. We're in the 2000 years of playing it out after He came. We're coming up on that 2000-year mark when He walked the Earth. We will see things accelerate over the next several years and to the end.

Genesis 6:6 is where God reveals Himself and what He's going through. He spoke to Enoch this way and Noah this way and was having these men go and preach and teach. God was grieved that He put man on the Earth. If you say you want to walk with God, you have to be a standard in a generation where that standard is not in existence or contested. That means you have to preserve your bloodline and genetics. It means you have to preserve the standard of God's word and what He's already proclaimed. He's not going to change His mind about anything.

❖ **Genesis 6:7 AMPC:**
So the Lord said, I will destroy, blot out, *and* wipe away mankind, whom I have created from the face of the ground—not only man, [but] the beasts and the creeping things and the birds of the air—for it grieves Me *and* makes Me regretful that I have made them.

- The Amplified version is a more accurate translation of the Bible as far as taking it from the Greek language into English.
- I learned this from one of my professors who said it was more accurate in the descriptive part.
- The Greek language is very descriptive, and English is one of the worst languages to translate.
- In this verse, God is so upset and adamant that He is using strong words to express His hurt.
- He wants to destroy, blot out, and wipe away mankind.
- God doesn't say He's going to destroy the Earth. He says, "I'm going to wipe away mankind, whom I have created from the face of the ground, not only man but the beast and the creeping things and the birds of the air, for it grieves me and makes me regretful that I had made them."
- The animals are mentioned because hybridization was occurring.
- Interbreeding was happening between species. It has to do with the serpent and satan being the god of this world now.
- He did this through the food source and water sources. I don't know exactly how it got in, but the serpent's seed got in. It also got into the animals.
- We see this in Greek mythology, the hieroglyphics, different writings, and the art made of half-breeds.
- Genesis 6 explains how the gods came down.

❖ **It is essential to know the details in Genesis to share with people so they can understand what they're dealing with today.**

❖ **The Lord was about to destroy all the animals too. Something happened with them that got Him so upset with everything.**

**What was God's response to an evil world?**
_____
_____
_____
_____

## FINDING FAVOR WITH GOD

❖ <u>**Genesis 6:8 AMPC:**</u>

But Noah found grace (favor) in the eyes of the Lord.

- Noah found grace or favor with God.
- When God looks at someone and doesn't look away, He stares at them, and they catch His gaze.
- What's happened is that they have caught His attention, and He doesn't look away. When He looks at you, He continues to stare. It's more than just a glance.
- It causes favor to come into your life because His heart goes out to you
- You can do certain things in this life that cause Him to stare at you, to catch His attention, and He doesn't look away immediately.

- That's what happened with Moses on the mountain. The Lord's favor was with him. Exodus 33:11 says, "He talked with God face to face."
- His gaze causes a transfer from His goodness to becoming part of you.
- That's why after so much time with the Lord on the mountain, Moses had the glory of God shone on his face. He had to cover his face around the people because they couldn't handle it. That was the favor of the Lord.
- It's because of association and walking with God that favor caused Moses to be above his brother.
- That's also what happened with Jesus.
- God anointed Jesus with the oil of joy above His brethren.
- It happened with Noah. Noah found grace and favor in the eyes of the Lord.

## JUST AND RIGHTEOUS

❖ **<u>Genesis 6:9 AMPC</u>**

This is the history of the generations of Noah. Noah was a just *and* righteous man, blameless *in* his [evil] generation; Noah walked [in habitual fellowship] with God.

- The word "*generations*" has to do with seed and bloodline.
- "Noah walked in habitual fellowship with God." That's the same statement spoken about Enoch.

- We've already learned about the lineage, and all God planned through these men's birth and living.
- We saw how Methuselah lived to be almost 1000 years old. That was a very long time.
- He lived up until the flood.
- These men lived a long time; some had favor and caught the attention of the Lord. It continues.
- Noah became the father of three sons.

**According to Genesis 6:8-9, what did God consider righteous about Noah? How did Noah walk?**

_____
_____
_____
_____

- ❖ <u>**Genesis 6:10 AMPC:**</u>

  And Noah became the father of three sons: Shem, Ham, and Japheth.

  - The three sons, Shem, Ham, and Japheth, were from the womb of Noah's wife.
  - Eve had three sons through the Godly line. Seth was the only one of the three through Adam that remained Godly. Then Noah had these three sons.

## GOD SEES CORRUPTION

❖ <u>**Genesis 6:11 AMPC:**</u>

The earth was depraved *and* putrid in God's sight, and the land was filled with violence (desecration, infringement, outrage, assault, and lust for power)

- These words were used to describe what God saw.
- Most of us have no concept of encountering assault and violence the way that Genesis 6:11 describes.
- *"Violence filled the earth; the land was filled with outrage, desecration, infringement, assault, and lust for power."*

**Describe what causes violence to generate according to Genesis 6:11.**

_____
_____
_____
_____

## SEEKING GOD AMIDST DEPRAVITY

**DISCUSSION:**

I wonder what it was like in the days of Noah. Was it the same as it was for me when I became born again and called by God to operate in the Spirit and to walk with Him but encounter warfare constantly from being in this realm? What was it about Enoch that God was so pleased with him that He took him? What did Enoch do that we should learn from him?

Enoch was a prophet, so he had a mantle and an anointing. To grasp this, you must realize that he had a teaching or doctrine he was following. He had something he was pursuing other than being a prophet. When you look at it, who teaches their son to walk with God that way? How did he learn how to do all this? Today, we have the Bible, the gifts of the Spirit, the fivefold ministry of the church, the Holy Spirit in us, not just upon us as the prophets had, and so much more than what Noah or Enoch had in their day. Yet they excelled or superseded what we can do. That puzzled me so much; therefore, Enoch became my favorite subject of all time.

Even though Paul has given us so much more as far as doctrine for the New Testament that we all live by, Enoch has been one of those people that just in some way has always motivated me to seek the Lord diligently. In the book of Hebrews, when Enoch is mentioned, it talks about how he pleased God and had so much favor (Hebrews 11:5-6). It says that without trust or faith, it is impossible to please God. About Enoch, and in this context, the author of Hebrews is talking about faith in Enoch. You must believe that God exists and "that He is a rewarder of those who diligently seek Him." That's what Enoch had. He sought God, and God is a rewarder of those who diligently seek Him. In context, it's talking about faith.

Noah was perfect, and most translations say he was perfect in his generation. He was a righteous man and was blameless in that evil generation, which means that there were acts of sin. Certain acts of sin, when committed, begin to rearrange or program your genetics. Drug abuse or certain drugs can alter your DNA. Certain lifestyles can damage your DNA because sin entered and made a deposit in your family line to which the next generation is exposed. If satan can get people to sin, there's a point where that sin causes a malfunction or a mutation in your body. It doesn't only affect you mentally, but biologically where the code in your DNA is changed. Because of that sin, it transfers through the blood to the next generation, so their children will have a predisposition. Because you may have abused your kidneys or liver or contracted a disease due to sin or abuse, it can be transferred and start a trend in your bloodline. That's where you see the same disease pop up, where it's not fair that a child being born hasn't done anything wrong to cause that, yet it comes up. That's how people inherit a curse or predisposition to a disease.

It's not right that satan can bombard us in our environment or with the wrong food or chemicals in our bodies that cause damage in our bodies. It is programmed mysteriously. It is transferred as a message into our DNA so that the DNA goes to the offspring, and then they grow up with the same thing. They didn't even have to commit to the sin for it to enter in. They have a broken-down immune system right away. That's what Noah was kept from. He didn't have the serpent's seed or blood in his lineage. The seven people in his family on the ark were not infiltrated in any way. They were perfect. The Bible says they were blameless and righteous, which caused them not to have anything in their generations or their genetics. Noah and Enoch habitually walked with God.

- ❖ **<u>Genesis 6:12 AMPC:</u>**

    And God looked upon the world and saw how degenerate, debased, *and* vicious it was, for all humanity had corrupted their way upon the earth *and* lost their true direction.

- The Lord looks to and fro throughout the whole earth to see if there is anyone He could encourage or empower in righteousness.
- He is looking for someone willing and able and walking with God.
- He looks for those people to encourage, fortify, or empower.
- If He looks on the earth and doesn't see anyone, that's a problem.
- That's what was happening here. It was much worse than it is today.
- Jesus said that the last days before and when He comes "*will be just like the days of Noah*" (Matthew 24:37 AMP).
- We see that it was degenerate, debased, vicious, and corrupted. Humanity had lost its true direction.

**Do you notice similarities between Noah's days and today? What can we do about it?**

_____
_____
_____
_____


## RIGHTEOUSNESS TRIUMPHS OVER EVIL

❖ **Genesis 6:13 AMPC:**

God said to Noah, I intend to make an end of all flesh, for through men the land is filled with violence; and behold, I will destroy them and the land.

- Even though Enoch prophesied this, Noah now knew it.

- He's being told, "All flesh was going to go."
- God will destroy them and the land; the only ones to survive are the eight people on the ark.
- Noah was righteous and blameless, and he found favor with God.

❖ **Even though there's not a lot written about him, Enoch was the first of four preachers to find favor with God. Enoch did certain things that caused God to look his way and stare at him.**

❖ **Certain things we do will catch God's attention. If you grab His attention and He knows you, then you will have favor. He will be with you, and you will see profound things. Every generation has people like Noah and Enoch.**

❖ **In these last days, the whole body of Christ is supposed to have favor. We are supposed to have supernatural finances, health, and abilities beyond anything anyone can explain.**

❖ **Paul said that "the goodness of God leads you to repentance" (Romans 2:4). Therefore, the goodness of God revealed in our lives to people will cause them to repent.**

**What kind of character did Noah have that he found favor in God?**

_____

_____

_____

_____


**What leads us to repentance, and what does righteousness for a Christian look like?**

_____

_____

_____

_____

## CHAPTER FIVE

# The Powers of the Coming Age

*If then you have been raised with Christ, seek the things that are above, where Christ is, seated at the right hand of God.*
—*Colossians 3:1 ESV*

**DISCUSSION:**

The Lord has impacted me in several ways, and I want to share these experiences with you. Several years ago, I was on an airplane with my wife. I had just flown for work, and it had been a long day. I met up with my wife in Phoenix, Arizona, and then the airplane went on to Seattle, where we lived. As I took a seat, Kathi got on the plane, and then she came and sat beside me. I was tired from flying all day because we would put in 10-12 hours a day, so I fell asleep. I thought I was awake because I felt someone walk down the aisle. I knew the flight attendants because I had just finished working, so when I opened my eyes, I expected to see one of the flight attendants. I was in the aisle seat, and my wife was beside me in the middle seat. However, when I opened my eyes, I didn't see the flight attendant; I saw an angel.

The angel grabbed me by the arm and said, "You've asked the Lord to show you." The Lord said, "Through this angel, I have come to explain your question in the book of Hebrews about the powers of the coming age. How once we have tasted of the blood of Jesus and forgiveness, the gifts of the spirit and the powers of the coming age if we were to fall away or to renounce Jesus, that there was no forgiveness or repentance for that sin" (Hebrews 6:4-6). The powers of the coming age are something we've already tasted. I was a little confused about that because I thought, *I don't know that I've tasted that, and if it's something I'm supposed to have already tasted, I want to know what it is.* I couldn't figure out what it was.

Elijah and Enoch, who are referred to as, "men of old," were taken to Heaven in their physical bodies are still there with their bodies. It's a profound thing. We don't see that happening anywhere else in the Bible. I was puzzled about Old Testament people being able to be translated or disappear like that. In the New Testament we have the power of God coming on the day of Pentecost. Is there something more to water baptism, or being baptized in the Spirit, or the baptism of fire, that John talked about; how Jesus baptized with the Holy Spirit and fire (Matthew 3:11)? I'm teaching you to read every word and glean from this because it's deeper than you think.

The angel said, "I've been given permission to show you and explain to you the powers of the coming age." Then, he yanked me out of my seat, and we flew. I thought we were flying down the aisle, but suddenly we were outside the aircraft at high speed. We were going away from the aircraft. I could see the aircraft as we were leaving it and descending at an arc down to the Earth. We were about 7 miles up, then we landed on the Earth at a high rate of speed and got to where we were walking on the Earth.

The first thing I noticed was that we were in a dense forest with a field-like opening coming up ahead of us. I immediately noticed that the air was much richer and had more oxygen. It seemed cleaner. Everything was different. As I progressed, I realized that I had gone back in time and was now back before the flood. I discovered that the air and everything about the Earth differed. The air was thicker, and there was more oxygen in the air. It was puzzling because I felt like I was there in my body. I didn't know how that was possible because I was sitting beside my wife on an airplane.

As we walked, I saw this individual ahead of us coming to a clearing. I saw him take a step, and his foot went over into another realm. There was a divide from that one step. As he took the next step, half of his body was in the other realm then his other foot followed. When that happened, the Spirit of God came and wrapped Himself around him, and he walked over. It was seamless, and you would have missed it if you weren't looking, except for the power that enveloped and wrapped around him like a whirlwind as it pulled him into the other realm. There was a shockwave in the physical realm that we were in, even though this was a vision. The shockwave was sent out and came back through the forest where we were standing, and the angel and I had to brace ourselves, so we weren't blown over or thrown down. He said, "These are the powers of the coming age; it's resurrection."

Then he took me to another time which ended up being on the other side of the flood during the time of Elijah. We didn't go back up; we went over to the other side of the flood; I saw Elijah, and somebody was standing there with him. A chariot came and separated him from that other person, which I assumed was his servant. A fire and whirlwind came and took him, and Elijah left.

That's when the angel explained this to me; that this is the powers of the coming age, that it was the resurrection of the dead, and that Jesus was the first-born. He was the one that was resurrected first so that we could be. He was the first of many. The angel explained this to me, handed me a scroll, and said, "Your calling is on here." He said, "It explains your whole calling and everything you need to know about what you're called to do." I was really interested, and I knew that he would have to take me back, so I felt the urgency that we would be leaving, but I wanted to look at it. I didn't look at it, but I asked him, "Can I keep this?" He said, "No, you're not permitted to take it with you. You can just look at it, but don't worry; it's in your Bible, in 2 Corinthians 5."

When I opened the scroll, it was the fifth chapter of 2 Corinthians. It talks about how we're supposed to be ambassadors and go forth and announce that the Lord has forgiven us of our sins through the blood of Jesus and to compel or request that people come in and repent. It also talks about being born again. It's in the 17th verse, which all of us know, but there was much more information there. Then he took me back and placed me in my seat again, but it was pretty forceful. We came in at a high rate of speed. As I came back into consciousness, the plane shook pretty hard, and it was exactly when he put me back into my body and back into the seat.

I don't know if I was out of my body or in my body like Paul said in 2 Corinthians 12:2-3. It was just so real to me. I say this because it was Enoch that I saw dressed in animal skins and walking alone in that clearing. Nobody was with him, and I remember thinking it was natural for him to walk over. It wasn't a big deal for him.

I thought about how no one knew that he would be gone forever. No one knew that he wasn't coming back. No one observed this. It just happened. At that point, I was sure about one thing, Enoch was a form of the church in these last days.

- ❖ The plan of God that Paul talks about is that through the church body, the manifold wisdom of God would be revealed to the powers in the Heavenly realms.
    - The powers that be would be shaken and judged by our lives and the revelation operating through us.
    - It says this is the mystery that's been revealed to us (Colossians 1:26).
    - I saw that it was the resurrection power given to us through the born again experience and the Holy Spirit coming on the day of Pentecost.
    - That power that we endured from on high; that is the resurrection power upon us and in us.
    - The same power that rose Jesus from the dead is dwelling inside of us, and it will quicken our mortal bodies (Romans 8:11).

## SEEKING AND TRUSTING

- ❖ Enoch sought God diligently (Hebrews 11:5). Then it describes faith, which is the word for trust.

    - You will seek Him diligently if you trust God and walk with Him habitually. It's going to be a deliberate process.

- We have experienced the powers of the coming age, which is resurrection power.
- Through this resurrection power, we will do exploits in these last days.
- We will walk with God and be rewarded for it.
- He rewards those who diligently seek Him (Hebrews 11:6). The reward for Enoch was that he was taken.
- He was literally snatched or grabbed quickly, just like I was grabbed from the airplane.
- It says he was grabbed and taken in a flash, which you wouldn't see if you weren't looking. That's how the church will be taken.
- The church will be taken in the twinkling of an eye.
- The trumpet will sound, the dead in Christ will be raised, and we shall be changed. There will be a resurrection (1 Corinthians 15:51-52).
- The dead in Christ shall rise first, and then those Christians who are alive will be snatched (1 Thessalonians 4:13-18).
- It's part of the doctrine of the church.
- There's a snatching, but it is a walk into the next realm because we pleased God so much and were diligent and walked with God.

**How do we seek God deliberately, and what does it have to do with trusting Him?**

_____
_____
_____
_____

**How has He shown you that you can trust Him?**

_____
_____
_____

**How have we experienced the powers of the coming age through His resurrection power?**

_____
_____
_____

## THE FAVOR OF GOD

- ❖ At the end of the age, we'll see exploits, miracles, signs, and wonders, and God will be with us in favor. In his generation, Enoch was taken out and kept from the diabolical condition of the earth.

  - The church will be taken out the same way.
  - There's a plan and purpose for all of us these days that we live.
  - These individuals lived in the Old Testament, and the years they lived and their lineage was all in sequence.
  - Their names mean something.
  - There's a prophetic utterance concerning the Gospel being preached through the names of the genealogy.

❖ God kept Methuselah alive. He was the oldest person that ever lived. He lived longer than Adam.

- Adam only lived 930 years.
- Enoch was snatched away, but Methuselah lived longer than Adam.
- God extended his life to fulfill prophecy because God told Enoch that his son Methuselah would live until the flood.
- Therefore, Enoch prophesied that.
- The prophecies that are still unfulfilled about the Second Coming and about all the things that are to happen until the church is snatched away or walks over must come to pass.
- We're all an integral part of that, just like the people that lived in the Bible were.
- Enoch wasn't on the ark, but you know that God could've extended his life, and he could've outlived his son, but God chose not to do that.
- That's why it's very important for you to preach the good news and make people aware that we're here for a reason.
- In our lives, how long we live and where we live are all part of a plan and a strategy.
- Enoch fulfilled all of that, and Noah was the one that was supposed to build the ark and be the one on the boat.
- Only eight people were kept perfect in their generations.

- ❖ It is imperative to know the personality traits of Enoch and Noah to see how they walked and lived and managed their life on earth with interbreeding hybrids and animals. It was so evil that God was determined to wipe out that race of people.

**What will God's favor be like in the coming age?**

_____
_____
_____
_____

- ❖ God's miracles, signs, and wonders will come forth in your life because the resurrection power that rose Jesus from the dead is in you.

  - That resurrection power is the power of the coming age.
  - We can experience the powers of the coming age.
  - Now that we've tasted and experienced it, the clocks have frozen.
  - Everything begins to slow down.
  - Time is on your side because God has put you in His time frame to function by the Spirit, not just in the flesh.
  - God has given this revelation to you so that you can take that resurrection power in you and allow it to manifest in your body and infiltrate your organs and every part of you.

- You will receive supernatural healing and revelation about why you're alive on earth, the plan and purpose that God will extend your life until His plan and purpose are fulfilled. You're not going to die early.
- You have the power of the resurrection inside of you to fight against the enemy, take your stand, and live a full life.
- Find out what your name means. Look up your lineages and see what's inside of you that God is trying to tell you.

❖ Enoch was a profound individual that lived in a day when it was so hard to live and walk.

- Imagine living amongst people that were half monsters and half supernatural beings.
- The dinosaurs were destroyed, and none of them crossed over. They were hybrids.
- It would have been a terrible time to be on the earth, always fearing for your life, of being murdered or attacked because of the violence that was on the earth.
- The crime rate was astronomical. Yet Enoch had supernatural protection.
- The sons of God had supernatural protection.

❖ **You will find favor, and that's how it will be in the days to come. People won't be able to explain why God is with you in such a mighty way, but that's how it will be as the church begins without spot or wrinkle.**

❖ We have to get ready for the bridegroom to come. It could be momentarily or in a few years

❖ We will finish our work here on earth and be noted in Heaven for changing history.

**What do we have in us that causes miracles, signs, and wonders to come forth in our lives?**

_____
_____
_____
_____

**What can the church do to get ready for the coming of the Lord?**

_____
_____
_____
_____

## **PRAYER**

Father, in the name of Jesus, I thank You for the power of Your blood. I thank You for the power of Your name and the power of Your word. I thank You, Lord, for the power of Your resurrection. I thank You, Lord, that just like Enoch walked in this resurrection and understood your favor, we walk in that resurrection power, the powers of the coming age. We thank You, Father, that Your people will encounter supernatural favor and a supernatural ability beyond their ability to explain. I thank You, Father, that their finances are being touched and healed in the name of Jesus. I thank You, Lord, that their bodies are being touched and healed in the name of Jesus. I thank You for supernatural wisdom and supernatural impartation in their relationships, and their coming and going into their neighborhoods, cities, and country. Father, let the power of Heaven be with the body of Christ in these last days. Let us know that we're going to finally get to the place where we take our last step on this earth and transfer over, Lord. I thank You for supernatural testimonies, Lord, that Your people receive healing and supernatural finances, Lord. In the name of Jesus. Amen.

## CHAPTER SIX

# God Rewards the Diligent

*Jesus replied, "You must love the Lord your God with all your heart, all your soul, and all your mind."*
*—Matthew 22:37 NLT*

**DISCUSSION:**

The rewards that are coming to you for everything you're doing for the Lord are due to your diligence in seeking Him. That is another aspect of the walk with Enoch because he understood that God is a rewarder of those who diligently seek Him (Hebrews 11:5-6). Enoch's personality was one of this nature. He walked with God and believed He was a rewarder of those who diligently sought Him. The author of Hebrews mentioned Enoch when he spoke about faith. Faith is an aspect of receiving rewards. Enoch pleased God because of his diligence and understood that God would reward those who were diligent.

## HE REWARDS THE STEADFAST

❖ **<u>James 1:12 ESV:</u>**

Blessed is the man who remains steadfast under trial, for when he has stood the test he will receive the crown of life, which God has promised to those who love him.

- There is a reward here.
- It says you must remain steadfast in the good times and under trial.
- Once we have stood the test of whatever we're going through, we will receive the crown of life God promised to those who love Him.

❖ **I believe that I will get the crown of life, but not only that, there's so much more in Heaven. The rewards I received from this life when I was there were the relationship and access I had to Jesus. That was what I wanted. I didn't want the mansion or gold and silver jewels; I knew I had received Him. I was considered a Levite.**

❖ The Levite's inheritance was not earthly riches, like the other tribes. The inheritance the Levites received was the Lord Himself (Deuteronomy 18:1-2).

- That is the highest form of reward.
- When you get to Heaven, all you want to do is sit and talk with Jesus.

- You don't care about your mansion or all these other things.
- Worldly things are not the same in Heaven.
- You think you're going to receive all this stuff, but you're not going to want to sit around and count your money or jewels or walk around your house.
- You will want to sit and talk with Jesus and be assigned to work for Him.
- I saw that whatever assignment He gave you in eternity was the highest honor and perfect for you. You wouldn't want to do anything else.
- I didn't ask to go to my mansion when I was in Heaven. I didn't see my mansion. It never came to me to ask Him. I never asked Him what rewards I would get.
- My reward was literally Him.
- That is the goal that we should have on the earth.
- We get the crown of life because God promised us this, but the crown of life is eternal life, which means that we have total access to God.
- Heaven has no time or distance and no reference points like on earth.

**How are we to remain under trial? What will we receive?**

_____
_____
_____
_____

## HE REWARDS THE HARDWORKING

❖ **<u>Colossians 3:23-24 ESV:</u>**

Whatever you do, work heartily, as for the Lord and not for men, knowing that from the Lord you will receive the inheritance as your reward. You are serving the Lord Christ.

- We are going to receive an inheritance as a reward for working for the Lord.
- Consider this verse, whenever you do something, even if you don't feel like you got paid back for doing it.
- We have to get out of this idea that we will have instant gratification or an instant reward for things.
- The idea of doing something and expecting to get a hundred-fold back for what you did, is limiting God because He wants to do much more than that, and He can do it in any way He wants.
- When I gave my bicycle away, I didn't expect 100 bicycles back, and I haven't gotten 100 bicycles back.
- Inheritance and rewards give you access.
- He is my inheritance. I'm going to get it all, but I can't just put my finger on one thing or another.
- It is much more than that; you don't want to limit the Lord.

**How do we receive the inheritance of God?**

_____
_____
_____
_____

## HE REWARDS US FOR WHAT WE DO

- ❖ **<u>Matthew 16:27 ESV:</u>**

For the Son of Man is going to come with his angels in the glory of his Father, and then he will repay each person according to what he has done.

- That is the reward system that we're talking about.
- Enoch knew he would receive his reward in his life on earth.
- He knew that there was another kingdom.
- Enoch was being translated back and forth according to his writings.
- He was at the throne, being transported all over the earth and having visions. He was constantly in both realms.
- This is the promise that we have, that God will come back and retrieve us, and we will be rewarded for what we have done.
- In everything you do, be mindful that angels are recording, and they will send that to the Lord.
- He will ensure you're rewarded for all your good deeds.

**How does God repay us, and when do we receive it?**

_____
_____
_____
_____

## HE REWARDS THE FAITHFUL AND TRUE

❖ **Matthew 25:21 ESV:**

His master said to him, 'Well done, good and faithful servant. You have been faithful over a little; I will set you over much. Enter into the joy of your master'

- I encountered this with the Lord, and then He sent me back. He said, "Well done, good and faithful servant." He said, "You've been faithful in the little." Then, He sent me back to do even more.
- It's part of the reward system.
- At Warrior Notes, we do as much as we can for people. We don't think about how much money we can get; we think about how much we can give.
- We think about helping people and how many books we can write, not to sell them, but to ensure everyone gets what they need.
- The Lord taught me to do as much as possible to help people with what I've been given.
- Do as much as you possibly can for Him because the Lord will give you a promotion, and you will oversee many more things in Heaven.

**How do we become rulers over much in Heaven?**

_____

_____

_____

_____

## HE GIVES TO THOSE WHO DELIGHT IN HIM

❖ **Psalm 37:4 ESV**

Delight yourself in the Lord, and he will give you the desires of your heart.

- Desiring things in your heart will always be there, but the way you get your heart's desires is to delight yourself in the Lord.
- Let your focus be on Him and be excited about Him.
- You have to want Him, not the things He can give you.
- Think about Him and the delight that He has for you. Delight in Him. Then He will give you the desire.
- You're going to be irresistible to Him. It's a fact.

**How can you personally delight yourself in the Lord and your relationship with God?**

_____

_____

_____

_____

## GOD THE REWARDER

- <u>**1 Peter 5:4 ESV:**</u>

    And when the chief Shepherd appears, you will receive the unfading crown of glory.

- <u>**Revelation 22:12 ESV:**</u>

    Behold, I am coming soon, bringing my recompense with me, to repay each one for what he has done.

- <u>**2 Corinthians 5:10 ESV:**</u>

    For we must all appear before the judgment seat of Christ, so that each one may receive what is due for what he has done in the body, whether good or evil.

- <u>**1 Corinthians 4:5 ESV:**</u>

    Therefore do not pronounce judgment before the time before the Lord comes, who will bring to light the things now hidden in darkness and will disclose the purposes of the heart. Then each one will receive his commendation from God.

- <u>**2 Timothy 4:8 ESV:**</u>

    Henceforth there is laid up for me the crown of righteousness, which the Lord, the righteous judge, will award to me on that day, and not only to me but also to all who have loved his appearing.

- ❖ <u>**Hebrews 11:6 ESV:**</u>

    And without faith it is impossible to please him, for whoever would draw near to God must believe that he exists and that he rewards those who seek Him.

- ❖ <u>**1 Corinthians 3:12-15 ESV:**</u>

    Now if anyone builds on the foundation with gold, silver, precious stones, wood, hay, straw—each one's work will become manifest, for the Day will disclose it, because it will be revealed by fire, and the fire will test what sort of work each one has done. If the work that anyone has built on the foundation survives, he will receive a reward. If anyone's work is burned up, he will suffer loss, though he himself will be saved, but only as through fire.

- ❖ <u>**Romans 6:23 NLT:**</u>

    For the wages of sin is death, but the free gift of God is eternal life through Jesus Christ our Lord.

- ❖ <u>**2 Peter 3:9 ESV:**</u>

    The Lord is not slow to fulfill his promise as some count slowness, but is patient toward you, not wishing that anyone should perish, but that all should reach repentance.

- ❖ <u>**Revelation 2:10 ESV:**</u>

    Do not fear what you are about to suffer. Behold, the devil is about to throw some of you in prison, that you may be tested, and for ten days you will have tribulation. Be faithful unto death, and I will give you the crown of life.

- Here, what seems to be a terrible end is really literally Jesus saying, "Just be faithful to the end, and you're going to get the crown of life, which would be far greater than the suffering."
- It is the balance that needs to be taught.

❖ <u>**1 Corinthians 15:58 ESV:**</u>

Therefore, my beloved brothers, be steadfast, immovable, always abounding in the work of the Lord, knowing that in the Lord your labor is not in vain.

❖ <u>**Matthew 25:14-18 ESV:**</u>

"For it will be like a man going on a journey, who called his servants and entrusted to them his property. To one he gave five talents, to another two, to another one, to each according to his ability. Then he went away. He who had received the five talents went at once and traded with them, and he made five talents more. So also he who had the two talents made two talents more. But he who had received the one talent went and dug in the ground and hid his master's money."

- The Lord expects us to double at least what is given.
- That's what these men did.
- Jesus told this parable and had this in mind.
- Part of the reward system is to produce fruit in keeping with repentance.
- It says he gave to each according to their ability.

- Some were given five, and some were given two, but it says it was according to their ability.
- You are only responsible for what you're given to produce with that.

**How and why is being a good steward important to God?**

_____
_____
_____
_____

- ❖ <u>**2 John 1:8 ESV:**</u>

  Watch yourselves, so that you may not lose what we have worked for, but may win a full reward.

- ❖ <u>**Matthew 6:6 ESV:**</u>

  But when you pray, go into your room and shut the door and pray to your Father who is in secret. And your Father who sees in secret will reward you.

- ❖ <u>**Hebrews 10:35 NASB:**</u>

  Therefore, do not throw away your confidence, which has a great reward.

- ❖ <u>**Ephesians 2:8 ESV:**</u>

  For by grace you have been saved through faith. And this is not your own doing; it is the gift of God.

- ❖ **Genesis 15:1 ESV:**

  After these things the word of the LORD came to Abram in a vision: "Fear not, Abram, I am your shield; your reward shall be very great."

- ❖ **Thessalonians 2:19 ESV:**

  For what is our hope or joy or crown of boasting before our Lord Jesus at his coming? Is it not you?

  - Paul was saying that the reward he would receive was his people. They were his reward.
  - I feel the same way toward you. It's a great joy to have all of you in the body of Christ.
  - Our reward is that you are not only in Christ but that you're being built up, maturing, and producing fruit. That's the greatest reward.
  - It's not financial gain or things that we have. These are all worldly things.
  - Paul had it right. He inherited a family and was excited about it.

**What is the greatest reward? How will it change the way you will live your life?**

_____
_____
_____
_____

❖ **Ephesians 6:8 NASB:**

Knowing that whatever good thing each one does, he will receive this back from the Lord, whether slave or free.

## THE TESTING BY FIRE AND THE NARROW WAY

❖ **1 Corinthians 3:10-15 ESV:**

According to the grace of God given to me, like a skilled master builder I laid a foundation, and someone else is building upon it. Let each one take care of how he builds upon it. For no one can lay a foundation other than that which is laid, which is Jesus Christ. Now if anyone builds on the foundation with gold, silver, precious stones, wood, hay, straw— each one's work will become manifest, for the Day will disclose it, because it will be revealed by fire, and the fire will test what sort of work each one has done. If the work that anyone has built on the foundation survives, he will receive a reward. If anyone's work is burned up, he will suffer loss, though he himself will be saved, but only as through fire.

- There will be many who don't find this narrow way.
- Many will suffer a loss on that Day, and some will be well-known people, well-known ministers, and well-known people claiming to be believers, but they had not built their lives on Jesus Christ.
- You're nothing if you don't have love.
- If you don't do things for the right reasons, you will suffer loss. That's how it is, but it's not being taught.

- God will reward you, but make sure you build on the foundation already laid.
- We must have an attitude: "According to the grace God has given you." That is what you must work with.
- We're not required to do something we have not been given to do.
- We need to be building on that foundation.
- Paul said, "I have a specific grace that was given to me, and so that's what I'm doing." That's how it was with Jesus.

❖ **When I was in Heaven, He talked to me. He didn't mention other people.**

❖ **I stood before the judgment seat of Christ; it was me standing before him, as I was shown what I had done with what I was given.**

**How do you find the narrow way?**

_____
_____
_____
_____

**What's the purpose of the fire, and how will you surrender to the Father and His righteousness?**

_____
_____
_____
_____

- ❖ <u>**1 Corinthians 3:8 ESV:**</u>

  He who plants and he who waters are one, and each will receive his wages according to his labor.

- ❖ <u>**Matthew 6:20 ESV**</u>

  But lay up for yourselves treasures in heaven, where neither moth nor rust destroys and where thieves do not break in and steal.

- ❖ <u>**Matthew 6:2 ESV:**</u>

  Thus when you give to the needy, sound no trumpet before you, as the hypocrites do in the synagogues and in the streets, that they may be praised by others. Truly I say to you, they have received their reward.

- ❖ <u>**Matthew 5:11-12 ESV:**</u>

  Blessed are you who when others revile you and persecute you and utter all kinds of evil against you falsely on my account. Rejoice and be glad, for your reward is great in heaven, for so they persecute the prophets who were before you.

- ❖ <u>**Revelation 3:11 ESV:**</u>

  I am coming soon. Hold fast what you have, so that no one may seize your crown.

❖ **2 Timothy 4:14 ESV:**

Alexander the coppersmith did me great harm; the Lord will repay him according to his deeds.

- Paul goes on to say that this man, who was a minister, was working against Paul's ministry.
- In other translations, it says *he was working against the ministry of the Lord,* and Paul said that the Lord would repay him, but it's not going to be good for that man.
- It's an example of people that work against other Christians.
- It is a terrible thing, but God remembers all of it, and they will be judged by it. It says, "The Lord will repay him according to his deeds."

**According to this verse, how does the Lord repay us?**
_____
_____
_____
_____

❖ **1 Thessalonians 2:19-20 ESV:**

For what is our hope, or joy or crown of boasting before our Lord Jesus at his coming? Is it not you? For you are our glory and joy.

- I know I've already mentioned this, but this is the finishing touch on what Paul said. He said, "You are our glory and our joy."

- We will find out that the highest reward we can receive is access to Jesus Christ and God and to His kingdom in an intimate way.
- That is higher than anything else that you can receive as a reward.

❖ **In Heaven, I didn't see my mansion. I didn't ask for it, nor did I see my reward because my reward was getting access to Jesus Christ.**

❖ **Paul says that all his people were his glory, joy, and reward. So remember that!**

**What matters most in this life and the next? How does this tear down any belief system we may have about money, mansions, and rewards?**

_____
_____
_____
_____

❖ **Colossians 3:24 ESV:**
Knowing that from the Lord you will receive the inheritance as your reward. You are serving the Lord Christ.

❖ **Galatians 6:9 ESV:**
And let us not grow weary of doing good, for in due season we will reap, if we don't give up.

- We must not give up in order to reap.
- We have to continue with this and stay in there.

## THE IMPERISHABLE REWARD

❖ <u>**1 Corinthians 9:24-25 ESV:**</u>

Do you not know that in the race all runners run, but only one receives the prize? So run that you may obtain it. Every athlete exercises self-control in all things. They do it to receive a perishable wreath, but we an imperishable.

- So continue in your race to the very end. You must exercise self-control and diligence and stay in there.

❖ <u>**Romans 2:6 ESV:**</u>

He will render to each one according to his works.

❖ <u>**Luke 6:35 ESV:**</u>

But love your enemies and do good and lend expecting nothing in return, and your reward will be great, and you will be sons of the Most High, for he is kind to the ungrateful and the evil.

❖ **Luke 6:23 ESV:**

Rejoice in that day, and leap for joy, for behold, your reward is great in heaven; for so their fathers did to the prophets.

❖ **Mark 9:41 ESV:**

For truly I say to you, whoever gives you a cup of water to drink because you belong to Christ will by no means lose his reward.

- No matter what you did, it was not insignificant but powerful.
- It doesn't matter if it's water that you give to someone, it's worth it, and there's a reward connected with it.

❖ **Matthew 19:30 ESV:**

But many who are first will be last, and the last first.

- I saw this with people you had put on pedestals, and unknown people surpassed them.
- Major ministries will be at the end of the line, and whoever is the least, whoever is serving, those are the people that will be exalted in place.
- You'll be surprised who's sitting close to Jesus at the table in Heaven at the wedding.
- It won't be the people that you think.

**How are your ideals and pedestals knocked down by these verses?**

_____
_____
_____
_____

- ❖ **1 Corinthians 2:9 ESV:**

    But, as it is written, "What no eye has seen, nor ear heard, nor the heart of man imagined, what God has prepared for those who love him."

    - I saw this to be true. It's going to be exponential.
    - You will be surprised at what you receive as a reward.
    - It will be over things that you thought were insignificant.
    - It's going to be so powerful.
    - Do something nice for somebody every day, and you'll be surprised when you get to Heaven.

**How does true love for God put us in righteousness? What is the reward?**

_____
_____
_____
_____

## OUR AGREEMENTS AND ACCOUNTABILITY

❖ **<u>Romans 4:4 ESV:</u>**

Now to the one who works, his wages are not counted as a gift but as his due.

- The reason that this verse is included is that you think that when you make an agreement to do something, you will get something in return. But this is not the way it is with God.
- With God, when you do something, not expecting anything in return, He gives you much more than if you would have demanded it.
- The way the world works is if you do this for me, I'll do this for you.
- Ministry has become the same way.
- It's become, "if you do me a favor, I'll do you a favor."
- Whatever happened to doing something because it's the right thing to do?
- Give because you want to give, and then God will reward you.

**How does God's kingdom work differently than ours? What is He built on?**

_____
_____
_____
_____

## THE GOOD SERVANT

- ❖ **<u>Matthew 25:23 ESV:</u>**

His master said to him, well done, good and faithful servant. You have been faithful over a little; I will set you over much. Enter into the joy of your master.

- I've already gone over this verse, but it needs to be emphasized.
- What you will receive in Heaven is based on what you did with what you had on earth.
- You got promoted and passed your test down here by being faithful in the little.
- It's a comparison to eternity and what God has for you. I can't wait to get to Heaven and start my new job.
- He's already shown me some of the things I'll be doing. I'm very excited about it. It's child's play on earth compared to Heaven
- You'll be in charge over certain things in Heaven because of your faithfulness on earth

- ❖ **<u>Matthew 6:16-18 ESV:</u>**

And when you fast, do not look gloomy like the hypocrites, for they disfigure their faces that their fasting may be seen by others. Truly, I say to you, they have received their reward. But when you fast, anoint your head and wash your face, that your fasting may not be seen by others, but by your Father who is in secret. And your Father who sees in secret will reward you.

- You will get a better reward for doing things in secret.

❖ **Matthew 6:3-4 ESV:**

But when you give to the needy, do not let your left hand know what your right hand is doing, so that your giving may be in secret. And your Father who sees in secret will reward you.

- When you give to people, your reward is essentially determined by being seen or unseen.
- Jesus says, "If you give to be noticed, that is your reward."
- The Lord will reward you for what you did in secret, which is a better deal.

**How does giving, in secret, change you? What is the reward?**

_____
_____
_____
_____

❖ **Jeremiah 17:10 ESV:**

I the Lord search the heart and test the mind, to give every man according to his ways, according to the fruit of his deeds.

- ❖ **1 Timothy 6:17-19 ESV:**

    As for the rich in this present age, charge them not to be haughty, nor to set their hopes on the uncertainty of riches, but on God, who richly provides us with everything to enjoy. They are to do good, to be rich in good works, to be generous and ready to share, thus storing up treasure for themselves as a good foundation for the future, so that they may take hold of that which is truly life.

## BEING RAPTURED IN CHRIST

- ❖ **1 Thessalonians 4:13-18 ESV**

    but we do not want you to be uninformed, brothers, about those who are asleep, that you may not grieve as others do who have no hope. For since we believe that Jesus died and rose again, even so, through Jesus, God will bring with him those who have fallen asleep. For this we declare to you by a word from the Lord, that we who are alive, who are left until the coming of Lord, will not precede those who have fallen asleep. For the Lord himself will descend from heaven with a cry of command, with the voice of an archangel and with the sound of the trumpet of God. And the dead in Christ will rise first. Then we who are alive, who are left, will be caught up together with them in the clouds to meet the Lord in the air, and so we will always be with the Lord. Therefore encourage one another with these words.

    - Enoch was caught up and raptured.
    - Paul instructed the Thessalonians that this would happen.
    - Essentially we are like Enoch on the earth right now and walking with Him.

- We could see the resurrection and be called forth if the Lord comes in our lifetime.
- If He comes, we would see people coming out of their graves; then we would be taken up.
- We would walk right over and be caught up into the Heavenly realms.
- It will be in a twinkling of an eye. It will be so quick. We anticipate this happening.
- Your reward is in the hand of the Lord.
- When He comes, we are going to receive our reward.
- We need to be mindful of this. I just believe that this has helped you.
- We expect a lot of fruit coming forth from the body of Christ because we're all students and ministers of the Gospel.
- We are one big family, and we want to see the Lord return in our lifetime.


**How are you enraptured in Him now on earth?**

_____
_____
_____
_____


**In what ways do you feel you can grow by walking with Christ as Enoch did?**

_____
_____
_____
_____

## PRAYER

Father, I thank You so much for all my students, all my partners, and all the believers around the world, our family. Thank You, Lord. You are strengthening each one with Your Holy Spirit right now. Thank You, Lord, that we have learned and heard Your Scriptures one after another about the rewards You have for us. There are so many in the Bible. I thank You, Lord, that each one is encouraged right now and that we are all built up and strengthened. I thank You, Father; we are all anticipating the catching away and that You are going to come back and take us, just like You took Enoch, as 1 Thessalonians clearly says. Thank You, Lord, that You are coming soon. Cause us, Lord, to produce fruit and cause the deluge of the Spirit to fill the earth with this great and final move of Your Spirit in Jesus' name. Amen.

# CHAPTER SEVEN

# God's Battle Strategies

*Commit your work to the LORD, and your plans will be established.*
*—Proverbs 16:3 ESV*

**DISCUSSION:**

The plans and purposes of God will be implemented in those who love and obey Him. We are in a war, and we have the battle strategies. God is involved in helping us with His angel armies. To the world, it will go the way of all the prophecies in the book of Revelation. It will play out just like that, but for those who believe, we will walk with God and be snatched out. We'll be taken; and walk right over, just like Enoch. Jesus is the commander of the angel armies. He is the head of all those armies, and at any given moment, He can beckon and call for those angel armies, and they will come. As His body on earth, we have authority in Jesus' name to call and ask for that help. We can see things happen in our lives even if God's will has chosen to go the way of the book of Revelation. We see everything that's going to happen on the earth, but we don't have to be part of that. We can walk with God, and He will take us at the proper time. He will come back for His body. I see Enoch as being a type of the church.

We're going to get into this word *strategy*. The word *strategy* is similar to the word *plan*. In times of war, secret plans are used to strategize and maneuver. If certain scenarios occur, they resort to plans A, B, C, or D. It's much like a chess game. They own a certain amount of moves. People that know how to play chess know all the scenarios. You might think it's random when you play a game, but there is predictability and strategy. If you become a professional at something, things become more predictable. God is that way with His foreknowledge and the Spirit of God knowing the heart of God.

God knows His plans, and the Spirit knows His plans, and the heart of God (1 Corinthians 2:11). The Holy Spirit can transfer that to us, and we can know the will of God. That's why we pray in the Spirit. The Spirit knows the will of God and will help us pray out that perfect will (Romans 8:26-27). Strategies have to do with this. In the Old Testament, the prophets knew the strategies of God, and they were just supposed to be obedient to the commands of the Lord. They sometimes did things that seemed somewhat strange, but it was all part of a strategy to outfox the enemy. That's what God wants to do for us.

- ❖ **<u>Proverbs 16:8-9 ESV:</u>**
  Better is a little with righteousness than great revenues with injustice. The heart of man plans his way, but the LORD establishes his steps.

  - Here, it's showing us how we can think through things and strategize, but the Lord interprets each step we take.
  - We have to ask ourselves where we are right now.

- Are we praying out the mysteries by praying in the Spirit? Doing this will help you to know the will of God and allow Him to dictate which steps to take and in which direction to go.

❖ **I allow God to tell me what He has planned and in what direction He wants me to go. Then, He gives me the first step; what to do, whom to call, or what to buy, and it begins a domino effect.**

❖ **That's how it was in the Old Testament with the prophets. They didn't know everything. They were just told what to do.**

❖ **We all need to get to that place where we're going to do what God tells us to do. It might only be one step. It might be to do something a certain way or a task that initiates it.**

**What adjustments do you need to make in your life to get in alignment with God and allow Him to order your steps?**

_____
_____
_____
_____

**How do our plans get in the way of what God is trying to accomplish in our lives?**

_____
_____
_____
_____

## YOUR STEPS ARE ORDERED

**DISCUSSION:**

God's timing is so important. I've been told things that were going to happen and what God wanted, but I didn't know the timing of it. We need to be careful not to initiate things too soon. Let God initiate your steps, and let Him talk to you. If you don't know what to do, do not do anything until He tells you. There is so much you can do, such as feed the poor and help others. You can teach and preach the gospel, and as far as individual guidance goes, allow God to initiate the conversation with you on the steps you should take. He wants to give you information about your steps while you minister to people (Psalm 37:23). You are supposed to be in the field, working for the Lord. When I'm out preaching, teaching, or praying, the Lord will nudge me in a certain direction, and I receive insight. If I don't know, I can't tell people what to do until I know myself. You have to get to that place.

- **Proverb 24:3-4 ESV:**
  By wisdom a house is built, and by understanding it is established; by knowledge the rooms are filled with all precious and pleasant riches.

- There's a lot hidden in this verse.
- Wisdom is the implementation of knowledge.
- You can be given a word, but the way you deal with that word is through understanding.
- Understanding is a strategy.
- When you are given understanding, God is getting you set up for a strategy.
- Understanding is established, and rooms are filled with precious and pleasant riches.
- Solomon saw that God would do this for him through wisdom.
- He implemented this through all these sayings that he wrote.

**How is a house built? How does God intervene?**

_____
_____
_____
_____

❖ **<u>Proverbs 21:5 ESV:</u>**

The plans of the diligent lead surely to abundance, but everyone who is hasty comes only to poverty.

- It is saying here that if you don't know what to do, don't run ahead and be hasty.

- What is it that God is nudging you in your heart over? Whatever it is, you need to allow that to unfold. Through your diligence, let God give you direction to lead you into that abundance.
- You are led by your diligence, but that diligence is something you do.
- If you don't know what to do specifically, then don't do anything until God tells you. It is part of the strategy.
- I have learned to say "I don't know" when they ask me what I know.
- People will put you on a pedestal and think that you know everything, but there's no way that God will share everything with you all at once.
- He's going to want you to walk by trust. He will want you to establish your way with Him so that if He doesn't say anything, you don't do anything.

❖ That is what happened with Saul. Saul was supposed to wait for Samuel to come and make the sacrifice, and he was late. Saul took it into his own hands and left the office of King and went into the office of a Priest, which he was not called to do.

- Saul lost the kingdom and his life because he didn't wait for the priest to come. He didn't wait on God.
- The strategy has to be that you will continue to do what you know you're supposed to do until God tells you otherwise.
- You can continue to distribute food to the poor and help people.
- You can continue to encourage people and do whatever it is you're called to do and know you are supposed to do.

**How do you prosper? What leads you to poverty?**

_____
_____
_____
_____

## LIVING SPIRIT LED

**DISCUSSION:**

Many ministries are formed out of making things happen on their own, and they are maintained out of that. Many Christians live their lives that way, but that is not how it's supposed to be. You're supposed to constantly sow into your spiritual life and let God dictate the timing. We arrived at Warrior Notes at the perfect time because our call was set for the events on earth right now

You're being prepared, educated, instructed, and mentored by what we put forth so that you can step into that at the proper time. I took all the generals' recordings, just like you are going to take our recordings and watch the courses repeatedly. That's what I would do. I would listen to CDs and videos 100 times over again to the point where I could preach the sermon better than they could. They're the ones that preached the original sermons. I did that because I was sowing into my spiritual life. That's the strategy we're talking about here. God will lead you into abundance because you're diligent, but don't be hasty because you can make missteps and end up in poverty or deficit.

- **Colossians 3:23-24 ESV:**

  Whatever you do, work heartily, as for the Lord and not for men, knowing that from the Lord you will receive the inheritance as your reward. You are serving the Lord Christ.

  - That is something that I had to think about every day at work.
  - When I would go to work, it wasn't considered in the church's eyes as being in the ministry, but I was in the ministry.
  - I was doing what God asked me to do.
  - I worked heartily for the Lord and not for men. I sowed into my future, and it was my job.
  - I didn't see it as working for a company. I saw it as working unto the Lord, and that is what Paul is telling the Colossians.
  - Whatever we do, we're supposed to do it unto the Lord. We are serving Him. That is how God used me in the strategy He had for me.
  - Your job is your pulpit. Your job is not your source of income, even though it's how you get paid. That's your mission field, and you're called to be there. Everyone in the body of Christ needs to get this.
  - You are at your job or profession or assigned to your location and family; it's all because you are in the ministry, and it's part of a strategy.

- **When I was at my job, I saw that I was being prepared for what I am doing right now. I had only been in the ministry for five years. It took over 40 years to get to where I am now.**

- ❖ I am learning more every day than I used to because the Lord is moving by the Spirit in such an amazing way in my life.

- ❖ Colossians is saying what God wants you to hear right now. Whatever you are doing, do it heartily unto the Lord and let Him instruct you because it all has its purpose for the plan of God.

**What do you think Paul means by working heartily for the Lord?**
_____
_____
_____
_____

**What is your reward?**
_____
_____
_____
_____

## FOLLOWING GOD'S PLAN

**DISCUSSION:**

At a certain point, God will move you into what you think you should be in right now, but only when you are ready for it. Then, He will put you into it, and it will be seamless. It will be very easy in comparison as your character is being built, which is what happened with Enoch. Enoch had to listen to God. He was being told to do certain things, and Enoch had to learn to obey God even when it hurt.

That personality trait of seeing and knowing what God was doing is what caused Enoch to stay in there. There were strategies involved because he was 65 years old when he began walking with God. Enoch walked with God the year that Methuselah was born. He was 65 years old when he had Methuselah. Then he walked 300 years with God after that. They all lived much longer than we do today, but 65 was still almost a child. It was like a teenager in comparison. With all of us, it's never too late. Allow God to move in your heart and see the strategy He has for you.

❖ **<u>Proverbs 19:2 ESV:</u>**

Desire without knowledge is not good, and whoever makes haste with his feet misses his way.

- As we discussed, here is another verse that teaches you not to be hasty.
- Your desire cannot be all that drives you.
- You have to have knowledge and understanding because if not, you will have missteps. That's what I believe Enoch had to learn.
- I believe that every person that's ever been used by God has to have understanding, and you can't just have passion, but knowledge, as well.
- You have to add to your knowledge and understanding.
- Desire is not enough to sustain you, especially in the type of atmosphere we are in now.
- It wasn't only a desire; Enoch had to walk with God, which kept him there.

- He had to be trained with the knowledge and then receive understanding.
- Both wisdom and knowledge have to be there (Proverbs 2:1-2).

**What will sustain you in today's world to move in what God's called you to do?**
_____
_____
_____
_____

**What did Enoch have to have to be equipped to walk with God?**
_____
_____
_____
_____

## FOLLOWING GOD'S COMMAND

❖ <u>**Mark 16:15 ESV:**</u>

And he said to them, "Go into all the world and proclaim the gospel to the whole creation.

- That was the command that Jesus gave to the disciples and the command that He gave to us.
- It's more like a commander saying, "That is the strategy, and this is what we're going to do."

- We have this command to preach the gospel and go into all the world and proclaim the gospel to all creation.
- It doesn't say for us to change people.
- It doesn't say to do miracles. It says for you to go and proclaim, and God will perform miracles and justify your words (Mark 16:20).
- He is going to back them up with signs and wonders following.

**How does God back you up when you preach or proclaim His Gospel?**

_____
_____
_____
_____

❖ **Proverbs 3:6 ESV:**

In all your ways, acknowledge Him and he will make straight your paths.

- Here is a pretty easy formula and basic Christianity.
- In all your ways, just acknowledge Him.
- Acknowledge that you are with Him, and He's with you.
- Wherever you're going, take Him with you. He's already with you.
- The equation shows that if you acknowledge Him, He will make your path straight, which is basic understanding.
- Enoch understood this. He acknowledged God. He respected and honored God in his life.

- That character trait caused a strategy to be implemented from Heaven, and his path was made straight.
- Enoch's path was obvious to him, and he had no doubts about it, and neither should we.


❖ <u>**Psalm 127:1 ESV:**</u>

Unless the Lord builds the house, those who build it labor in vain. Unless the Lord watches over the city, the watchman stays awake in vain.

- This verse talks about strategy.
- It's talking about the Lord. He's the architect
- He's the one that began the whole project. He's the one who'll finish it.
- Those who build the house must do it unto the Lord, or the builders build in vain.
- If you won't involve the Lord and acknowledge Him in your ways, it says here, "It's vain for the watchman to stay awake. It's in vain for the builders to show up if the Lord's not in it."
- Enoch wasn't doing this for himself.
- Noah wasn't doing it for himself.
- Four generations of preachers, beginning with Enoch, ministered and went around and preached righteousness.
- It would be in vain if God did not lead them.
- We have to know the plan of God.
- Paul told us that the mystery had been revealed in this time that we live, and that is Christ in us.

- Through the church, the manifold wisdom of God will be made known.
- That's all that we're supposed to be doing right now.
- The strategy has already been revealed. The mystery has been hidden, but now it's been made known.
- We're not going to do things on our own.
- We're going to make sure that the Lord's building the house.

**According to Psalm 127:1, how is God's way the better way?**

_____
_____
_____
_____

**How often do we see people do ministry and God's work in vain in their own strength, and how do we avoid this from happening?**

_____
_____
_____
_____

## MAN'S FOLLY CAUSES HIM RUIN

❖ **Proverbs 19:3 ESV:**

When a man's folly brings his way to ruin, his heart rages against the Lord.

- That's what has been happening to people. They're angry at the Lord then they become angry at you and each other.
- It's because they're not walking in the ways of the Lord.
- They're not allowing God to reveal His battle strategies to them; instead, they're wandering. The Bible calls this folly.
- When people are tripping up and doing their own thing or trying things out, but they have no purpose, plan, or strategy that God has given them, it's called folly.

❖ "A man's folly brings his way to ruin." A person who calls themselves a Christian but is randomly trying seven different things and says the chances are that one of them will work is living by the ways of the world.

- There's nothing random about the ways of the Lord. It's all strategy.
- You have to have this mindset.
- That is how people fail. I see this happening in Christians and the world. Then his heart rages against the Lord.
- It's silly that when you make a mistake, you blame the Lord for it, but He was not in it
- God would never allow you to fail.
- He wouldn't send you into something to fail.
- He wouldn't say, "Here's what I want you to do," and then not have it happen. That is not how God works.

❖ So, what are you blaming God for? Do you think that He would set you up for failure? That was something Enoch had to get over.

- Enoch wasn't like Jonah. Jonah felt like God set him up for failure because the city repented, and that wasn't part of what he thought was going to happen
- God gave an ultimatum. Judgment was coming in a certain amount of days if they didn't repent (Jonah 1-4). Jonah figured these people were vile and wouldn't repent, and he was mad when the people did repent.
- Enoch had to have all that burnt out of him to where he just delivered.
- Enoch didn't walk in missteps. He didn't see ruin because he was just being obedient
- His heart wasn't mad at God in any way, even though it was much worse than the time of Jonah and much worse than our time.
- It's a character trait.
- God has plans and purposes that He tells His people to be part of.
- He tells us all to be part of that, but He's not setting it up for failure.
- He's not planning on failing. I believe that we can walk as Enoch did once we get this.

**What is considered a folly? List some from the points and then list a couple of other examples.**

_____
_____
_____
_____

❖ **Jeremiah 29:11 ESV:**

For I know the plans I have for you, declares the Lord, plans for welfare and not for evil, to give you a future and a hope.

- I know the plans or the battle strategies I have for you, declares the Lord. Plans for welfare or prosperity and not for evil, to give you a future and a hope. This is the God that we serve.
- He has plans and purposes for us, and we will succeed.
- A future, a hope, plans for us to prosper, and this is the God we serve.
- That is the way Enoch saw God. That was all part of Enoch's personality.
- Everyone who was cleansed and purified to be a voice in their generation had to get to this place in their person.

**How can we know that God is dedicated to seeing us prosper by this verse?**

_____
_____
_____
_____

## DISCERNING GOOD AND EVIL

❖ **Genesis 3:5 ESV:**

For God knows that when you eat of it your eyes will be opened, and you will be like God, knowing good and evil

- We have to have the discernment to know when something is being said and whether or not it is God and His plan.
- God will show you His strategy for your life and the plan He has for you, but you have to base it on Scripture; then, if anything contrary to that comes, you will know and say that *it isn't of God.*
- Even though it looks like it's God, it may not be God.
- You have to be able to eliminate what is false.
- That's where Eve should have said no and walked away, but she didn't.
- She didn't discern what was being said and that God would know if she ate of it; her eyes would be open.
- Adam and Eve's eyes were already open, but God never wanted them to know evil.

❖ They didn't have the controversies that we have today within us. We weren't opposing ourselves by having struggles. The struggle in this world is that we know evil. It's a seducing spirit that causes us to struggle with doing good.

- It was never God's plan for us to know evil.
- Adam and Eve were already like God. They didn't need to know good and evil. They only needed to know good.
- The battle strategies of the Lord and the plans of the Lord were for us never to know evil but to know the truth and God's plan so well that we would spot anything that was a misstep.
- When you deal with people who claim that they're working for God or God's telling them something, you have to be able to discern in your heart what's right and what is not.

- That is what Eve should have done and Adam as well.
- As children of God, we need to receive this impartation that God has a plan and strategy for your life and the body of Christ.
- We should be so well versed in it that the Spirit of God can stand up and verbalize if a person is speaking by the Spirit.
- People are saying so many things audibly, and it is not always God. That is not how it's going to go.
- Christians are walking in deception, and they're spreading it around.
- Even if it's unintentional, it's still wrong.
- Be convinced that God has a strategy.
- Allow the impartation from these verses we've discussed to permeate your being right now.

**What is the struggle in this world?**

_____
_____
_____
_____


**Like Adam and Eve, what are we supposed to know of? How do we get back to truth?**

_____
_____
_____
_____

**How do you know when you are following God's plan and strategy?**

_____
_____
_____
_____

**How can we discern if someone is speaking by the Spirit of God?**

_____
_____
_____
_____

## PRAYER

Father, in the name of Jesus, I thank You so much for everyone in the family of God. I thank You that the power of the Holy Spirit is coming upon everyone, and they are receiving an impartation of your battle strategies and plan for each individual. I thank You that You're going to speak by the Spirit right now profoundly to each individual and that they will receive instruction, wisdom, and understanding in all Your ways and what You have for them in the name of Jesus.

# CHAPTER EIGHT

# The Intensity of Serving God

*And whatever you do, in word or deed, do everything in the name of the Lord Jesus, giving thanks to God the Father through him.*
—*Colossians 3:17 ESV*

**DISCUSSION:**

Anyone that's ever been used of God carries an intensity about them. It's a character trait that we find with Enoch, not only in his writings but also in the brief encounter that I had with him. He appeared to be very intense and focused. Intensity is really the word for *focus*. We should also have the character traits Enoch has in this time that we live as the Church. Being focused will cause you to stay on course and keep the attitude you need to acquire what God has asked you to do. You have to acquire it. It won't just come to you.

❖ <u>**1 John 3:8 ESV:**</u>

Whoever makes a practice of sinning is of the devil, for the devil has been sinning from the beginning. The reason the Son of God appeared was to destroy the works of the devil.

- The reason the Son of God appeared was to destroy the works of the devil.
- The devil is very intense, and he habitually sins.
- Through John, God says that the devil makes a practice of sinning and has done it from the beginning.
- He also says that those who make a practice of sin are of the devil, and he is talking to Christians.
- Unfortunately, we can't eliminate this fact. Many people have tried to, but the Scriptures were written to the church.
- The apostles and those that wrote the Bible are talking to believers.
- John is saying that if you practice sin, you are of the devil.
- You are either of God or of the devil.
- 1 John is not a very popular book because he was so intense.
- You can imagine what Enoch was like in the world that he lived in.
- John was very black-and-white with his words. There were no gray areas or lukewarmness like we see today.
- The enemy is after Christians. In fact, he is after everyone.
- He doesn't change, and he is very intense.
- Most of us need to step it up a few notches and be like Enoch.

❖ Walking with God meant Enoch was intense, focused, and on target with the Lord. From what I gather in his writings, he would disappear and be translated often. Enoch was being translated a lot right before he disappeared permanently.

- It wasn't like it just happened once; he went back and forth from the physical to the spiritual realm.
- It needs to be taught, and you need to be made aware of this.
- I'm imparting this to you because the devil has been sinning from the beginning. The devil doesn't back off, so we need to be more intense.
- God is saying through John that the reason Jesus, the Son of God, appeared was to destroy the works of the devil.
- He wasn't sent to hinder them, slow them down, or push them aside but to destroy them.
- To destroy something means it does not exist anymore. It's not able to be used any longer. That's what Jesus did, and that's pretty intense.
- John is intense. Jesus' assignment was intense, and our assignment is intense, just like it was for Enoch in the day he lived.
- Jesus appeared to destroy the works of the devil, so how much more are we supposed to be enforcing that right now?

❖ **The church is supposed to be rising up at least a couple of notches more than where she is right now.**

❖ **She's the bride, but she's also the one that the gates of hell cannot prevail against. That's who Jesus was.**

❖ **He wants us to be hot, just like the apostles were, and Enoch was.**

**How do you stay on course with what God has asked of you?**

_____
_____
_____
_____

**How is one on the side of the devil with their actions?**

_____
_____
_____
_____

**How was Enoch in the way he walked with God?**

_____
_____
_____
_____

**What was Jesus' assignment, and how has that become our assignment as well?**

_____
_____
_____
_____

## A CHOSEN GENERATION

❖ <u>**1 Peter 2:9 ESV:**</u>

But you are a chosen race, a royal priesthood, a holy nation, a people for his own possession, that you may proclaim the excellencies of Him who called you out of darkness into his marvelous light.

- Heaven is very intense. It's really bright, and it's like that everywhere in Heaven.
- When you look into the sky, there is no other light source like the sun.
- The brightest and most intense time of the day on earth is how it is in Heaven always.
- In Heaven, when you look up, God is the source of light, but His light is everywhere.
- There is no darkness in Heaven, and there are no shadows anywhere.

**DISCUSSION:**

When I was in Heaven, walking on a walkway in paradise, I could not see a shadow no matter what, even though there were trees. Everything in Heaven is like the Earth, only it's much better. Nothing casts a shadow, so that means that light is everywhere. It just didn't come from a certain source. That's the intensity of Heaven. Light penetrates the darkness, and it pushes darkness out. That's what it should be doing in your life. You should not be dealing with some of the things you're dealing with. You have to ask why they're happening. Peter said, "We're a chosen race." We're chosen as a race of people, and we are a royal priesthood. We are priests, but we are royalty. Two parts are being used together, a royal priesthood and a holy nation. That means we are set apart. It's for His own possession.

In Heaven, I saw that holiness was ownership. It's not behavior; it's that we've been bought, and we're owned. We are God's own possession. If you comprehend this, then you're going to function with intensity. You're not going to be diluted or compromised. You're not going to be lukewarm. It says in this verse, "that you may proclaim the excellencies of Him who called you out of darkness into his marvelous light," so you need to proclaim them. You need to walk out of the darkness. You need to do something. You are called out of it, but you will have to walk out of it.

It's the experience of being born again, baptized in the Holy Spirit, fed God's word, and encountering the powers of the coming age and the blood of Jesus; it has to mature you. You have to get to the place where Enoch was and walk with God in intensity. We need more intensity and more focus within the body of Christ. It's time to allow the Spirit of God to take us into this place. It all begins with the born again experience.

- ❖ **2 Corinthians 5:17 ESV:**
  Therefore, if anyone is in Christ, he is a new creation. The old has passed away; behold, the new has come.

  - All of Heaven has cooperated in the plan of God.
  - It has already been implemented.
  - Here, it says that once we're born again, we are in the plan of God.
  - We are in the perfect will of God as believers, but the world is not.

- We need to preach the gospel, but for all of us, this has already happened
- We have become new. We are a new creation, which means that nothing of the old exists anymore.
- It has all passed away, and the new has come.
- With that newness, we have a sharpness about us.
- We have the ability to focus on the truth, which causes us to walk in it.

**What does Scripture tell us about our newness in Christ through the born again experience?**

_____
_____
_____
_____

**How do you come out of the dark and into the light?**

_____
_____
_____
_____

❖ <u>**1 Kings 16:18 ESV:**</u>

And when Zimri saw that the city was taken, he went into the citadel of the king's house and burned the king's house over him with fire and died.

- This verse talks about intensity.

- It was a response to God doing something.
- When Zimri saw that the city was taken, he went in and finished his part of it and burnt the king's house.
- It says he "burned the king's house over him with fire and died."
- It's an example of the intensity in people that were part of what God was doing.
- They step in with intensity to act at a certain time.
- Samson was like that as well.
- With Samson, the Spirit of the Lord came upon him, and the intensity of that moment caused him to act.
- I want to see the intensity of people in the days to come.
- The old has passed away, but the new has come, which means the life we live now has to be intense.
- We must enforce what Jesus did on the cross and what He did with the devil's works.
- He destroyed the works of the devil, and we need to enforce that.
- We need to follow through as Zimri did.

**What are we called to enforce like Zimri? Like Jesus?**

_____

_____

_____

_____

## WORKING THEN RESTING

❖ **<u>Genesis 2:1-3 ESV:</u>**

Thus the heavens and the earth were finished, and all the host of them. And on the seventh day God finished his work that he had done, and he rested on the seventh day from all his work that he had done. So God blessed the seventh day and made it holy, because on it God rested from all his work that he had done in creation.

- It's the same with us; we need to work at what we're supposed to do and are called to do. Then that rest will come.
- Hebrew 4:3a ESV says, "For we who have believed enter that rest." Therefore, we're supposed to enter into that rest.
- Jesus said we are to work while it's still day; because night is coming when no one can work (John 9:4).
- When you can proclaim the gospel, you should do it.
- There's an intensity of knowing when to implement and do things at the right time. That time is now.
- Right now, while we can still preach the gospel and move about, we should.
- We've gone through times of restriction with diseases and calamities, but when we're not restricted, we should work.
- We should be intense when given the opportunity because that opportunity could be taken away.
- We must discern it, and then we can take advantage of it.

- So that's what intensity does: knowing when it's time to work and move about.
- God did that. He created for six days, and then He rested.
- That's what we do. We are intense enough to know that there's a time for resting and there's a time to work.
- Now is the time for us to work and get in the field and preach the gospel.
- We need to help as many people as we can and bring the light of the gospel to them.
- That intense, bright light dispels the darkness in every city and town we go to. That's what we are to do.

**What are the principles of working? And the principles of resting?**

_____
_____
_____
_____

**What should we be doing right now in our Day?**

_____
_____
_____
_____

## THE END OF DAYS

- ❖ **<u>Revelation 11:19 ESV</u>**:

    Then God's temple in heaven was opened, and the ark of his covenant was seen within his temple. There were flashes of lightning, rumblings, peals of thunder, an earthquake, and heavy hail.

    - What a scenario that John saw in the book of Revelation.
    - God's temple was open, and it revealed what was happening.
    - It is set to happen in the future, but it's for now, too.
    - It's all happening in Heaven.
    - The Ark of the Covenant was seen when the temple in Heaven was opened.
    - There were lightnings, rumblings, peals of thunder, earthquakes, and heavy hail.
    - It's all part of what John saw in the end times. I want to focus on the intensity.
    - Many intense things are going on in Heaven and in the throne room.

- ❖ Christians want to be entertained, have fun, and do activities, and that's good in its time, but when you look at what Enoch was going through, he had to have intensity because it was time for him to do what he was called to do. That's how it is in Heaven.

- I saw that there will be a time when we will be given rewards and get to rest. I saw the intensity of Heaven and how we really don't have much time left here.
- Many people don't need to go to hell; they need to go to Heaven. We need to help them and let them know.
- The only way to do that is to get out there and preach.
- I saw the intensity of this in Heaven in the throne room.
- Enoch was so intense because he was operating in both realms, and that was not an easy thing to do.

❖ Many people want to have fun but don't know what they're passing up on the earth. It's not all about retirement, having fun, or working hard during the week to have the weekends off to be entertained.

- I see it as not being aware of eternity or knowing what's going on in Heaven.
- People are just waiting for Jesus to come back, which has gotten us into a lot of trouble and why nobody is moving forward.
- They don't know the intensity that is in Heaven.
- Once you arrive at this place of intensity and do it for a while, it's easy and becomes second nature.
- Professionals in their jobs find it easy to operate in what they know, but it's not easy for you.

- Think about how it used to be in the beginning for you in your profession.
- Whatever you do, once you do it so many times, it becomes second nature, and it's no longer difficult.

❖ **The Lord showed me that the church should operate as Enoch did in these last days. It's revealed all through the prophecies.**

❖ **In the end days, there will be supernatural events, signs, and wonders, and the people who know their God will do exploits and see miracles.**

❖ **We are going to see a move of God like never before. It will come through those who are listening to these character traits that the Spirit wants to teach you.**

❖ **It will be how the men and women of old operated and walked in faith. Enoch completely abandoned himself. He was raptured up in God and didn't have his own will anymore.**

❖ **That's what I saw about Enoch, and that's what I saw God trying to do with everyone. He wants everyone to be won over to where they're walking with Him without hindrance.**

**What are some of the things that will happen in the end times?**

_____
_____
_____
_____

**What should we be doing to help people?**

_____
_____
_____
_____

## PERSECUTED FOR HIS SAKE

- **Hebrews 11:35-37 ESV:**

    Women received back their dead by resurrection. Some were tortured, refusing to accept release, so that they might rise again to a better life. Others suffered mocking and flogging, and even chains and imprisonment. They were stoned, they were sawn in two, they were killed with the sword. They went about in skins of sheep and goats, destitute, afflicted, mistreated—

    - This passage in the faith chapter of Hebrews doesn't seem to make sense based on how faith is being taught, but there is an aspect of faith where you're persecuted and suffer for it.
    - Certain people had chosen to die for the sake of Christ, and it says right here that others refused to accept their release, and they wanted to die as martyrs.

- They wanted to go to Heaven and were willing to stay in the situation, refusing to be released. Some people were stoned for their faith.
- Terrible things happened to certain people for their faith.
- Faith goes way beyond.
- In this country, we haven't been persecuted the way believers are in other countries.
- If that ever happened, you would understand that faith isn't based only on deliverance from a situation.
- Sometimes people go through things and die for the sake of Christ, which is part of the faith.
- These people were mentioned and rewarded for that, for staying in there and not accepting this because they wanted to have a better resurrection
- They wanted to be rewarded for being a martyr, essentially.
- It's a little negative, but it's in the Bible, and there is a balance to it.
- Sometimes we will suffer for what we believe.
- It's not a popular message, but it needs to be spoken.

**Have you ever suffered for believing in Jesus? How did you navigate through that? If not, what do you think about persecution on any level?**

_____
_____
_____
_____

## HONORING GOD AND PEOPLE IN HIS TEMPLE

- ❖ **1 Timothy 3:15 ESV:**

  If I delay, you may know how one ought to behave in the household of God, which is the church of the living God, a pillar and a buttress of the truth.

  - Paul instructs Timothy, saying, "If I don't come to you right away, just know how one ought to behave in the household of God."
  - Paul is saying he might be coming, but he may be delayed.
  - Paul would come to churches and discipline people.
  - He was trying to tell Timothy, who was being trained by Paul as a pastor, to teach the people how to behave in the household of God.
  - The household of God is the church of the living God, a pillar and a buttress, or a stronghold of truth, which means that your behavior will be affected either by evil or by the truth.
  - He told Timothy to make sure that people understand if he's delayed, that there is a certain way to behave in the household of God.
  - It's intense how Paul was delivering this message.

- ❖ Today we see the behavior of Christians acting inappropriately. It's because they don't have the intensity of Heaven within them to know.

  - Paul would not have put up with many things I see happening in the church today.
  - Paul wouldn't put up with it if he were over Warrior Notes.

- Paul would be calling things out and saying much more than I say.
- He was being more corrective than I am.
- I'm preaching Paul's gospel.
- If you read his writings, he didn't hold back.
- He would talk about people and say they'd done him great harm. He would say, "May God deal with him on the Day of Judgment."
- He called out their names.
- He called out a person's name and said they were working against his ministry; he would have nothing to do with them, and they would face judgment on the day of Christ. Paul was very intense.

❖ You can imagine an Old Testament prophet like Enoch and what it was like to be around him. He would say things like, "No, we're going to do things the way God told us to do them."

- I'm sure Enoch walked alone. I don't know that he had anyone with him.
- He may have had an assistant with him, but it was probably hard to get along with him because he was so intense at times. Elijah was that way.
- Jeremiah, Ezekiel, and Isaiah probably didn't have a lot of friends.
- They were very intense individuals and weren't into being entertained and doing all the things we do today.
- They were probably too intense for most of us to be around.
- The point is that Timothy had to learn to be that way in Paul's absence.

**How was Paul training Timothy to be? How can we learn from his example?**

_____
_____
_____
_____

- ❖ **Colossians 2:15 ESV:**

    He disarmed the rulers and authorities and put them to open shame, by triumphing over them in him.

    - We as ministers should be very intense regarding spiritual wickedness in the heavenly realms, which is what I see lacking in understanding for ministers and believers as well.
    - If Jesus did this and they're disarmed, we need to take our stand and enforce this. We need to continually disarm and remind the spirits that they *are* disarmed. I don't see this kind of aggressiveness anymore.
    - I see people as lukewarm at best.
    - God isn't serving leftovers or warm meals. He wouldn't do that when we could have a hot, fresh meal every day by the Spirit.
    - I see ministries abusing their privileges and position by not remaining intense about spiritual warfare.
    - Enoch understood all this. He understood what he was doing and went up against the evil God had to destroy.

- ❖ **I believe I'm more intense than most people and certainly more than most ministers, which makes me feel left out at times. I have a mandate that I feel others don't really understand.**

- ❖ **To show you the intensity of the warfare I saw, you need to grasp Colossians 2:15.**

**Why do you think ministers are overlooking spiritual wickedness operating in the church? What should our stance be concerning this?**

_____
_____
_____
_____

- ❖ <u>**Philippians 3:1-4 ESV:**</u>
  Finally, my brothers, rejoice in the Lord. To write the same things to you is no trouble to me and is safe for you. Look out for the dogs, look out for the evildoers, look out for those who mutilate the flesh. For we are the circumcision, who worship by the Spirit of God and glory in Christ Jesus and put no confidence in the flesh—though I myself have reason for confidence in the flesh also. If anyone else thinks he has reason for confidence in the flesh, I have more.

  - Paul goes on to talk about all of his qualifications, being circumcised, and his Hebrew roots.
  - He talks about how our confidence should be in the Spirit and the things of the Spirit, not in the flesh. He was calling certain people out.

- We see the same thing today in ministry and denominations and with people that control people.
- They're putting confidence in things rather than being spiritual.
- They control people into joining the church, saying that you have to do certain things for the church, give a particular amount of money, and then put restrictions on you.
- Paul is saying to put no confidence in the things of the flesh.
- He warns us to beware of the people doing these things because we're supposed to worship God by the Spirit.
- Paul said, "By the Spirit of God and the glory in Jesus Christ put no confidence in the flesh."

❖ Paul told the Philippians, "look out for dogs, evildoers, and those who mutilate the flesh." He was talking about the Jewish religion, the Hebrew teachers, and the Jewish people coming in and telling them that they still had to adhere to all the laws even though they were Christians now.

- He called that the denomination of the day. He called them dogs and evildoers.
- He called them out and said, "To write the same things to you is no trouble to me and is safe for you." He was very intense.
- Paul was writing these letters to all the churches in an intense way of wanting to be the person who was faithful in oversight.
- He was faithful as an apostle over all these churches but did not hold anything back.

- He was calling things as they were and telling the people that if they try to control them, they're evil doers. He said they're dogs.
- If somebody does not adhere to the gospel message, they need to go. They need to stay away from the people who have come and want to adhere to the teachings God gave through these men and women.
- Paul was protecting the people. He was a true father and apostle.

**How should we be exposing evil?**

_____
_____
_____
_____

**What should we be doing in our own time? As ministers? As the Church?**

_____
_____
_____
_____

## LIVING OBEDIENTLY

❖ **Philippians 2:12 ESV:**

Therefore, my beloved, as you have always obeyed, so now, not only as in my presence but much more in my absence, work out your own salvation with fear and trembling.

- Here is another intense scripture.

- Paul is saying they have always obeyed, but they should not just do this when he's around but live this way even more in his absence."
- He said to "work out your own salvation with fear and trembling."
- That doesn't sound like anything you hear today. That's how intense Paul was.
- When I was in Heaven, Jesus said, "You have to make every effort to stay in there with me." He told me things like that all the time.
- He would say, "Stay in there with Me; it's going to get hard, but just stay in there with Me."
- Jesus is so intense. It's hard to describe Him because He's so kind but also intense.
- He is very much in command and control.

**According to Philippians 2:12, what are we to do?**

_____
_____
_____
_____

**PRAYER**

Father, I thank You for the impartation of the Spirit. I thank You that You are intense light, that You are intense in your personality and truth. I thank You, Lord, that this causes us to be hot. It causes us to change. I thank You for all my students, all the believers in my family, Lord, that You will cause them to triumph over their enemies and that they will have the intensity and the power of the Spirit of resurrection in their lives, in Jesus' name, Amen.

# CHAPTER NINE

# The Bold and Righteous Ones Persevere

*For the righteous will never be moved;*
*he will be remembered forever.*
—*Psalm 112:6 ESV*

**DISCUSSION:**

Everyone should be made aware that in Heaven, people are really bold and fully convinced of everything. When I was in Heaven, everything was complete and very visible. No one was backward or shy. Everyone is bold. I was surprised at how sure everyone was in Heaven. I want to talk about this because the church in the book of Acts prayed for boldness, and God gave that to them, and they were persecuted. We think about what it would be like to live in the book of Acts and think about the Spirit of God coming on the day of Pentecost. You have to realize that many people hated Christians at that time, and they had to hide at times because they were being thrown in jail. Can you imagine what it was like for Enoch in the old days, before the flood? A lot was going on in the world with hybridization and animal interbreeding.

God said there was no one left that had not interbred. They were all wicked and evil. He said He was going to destroy the Earth and all of mankind. Everyone was going to die, and all the animals would die. He saved eight people on the Ark, but this was out of millions of people that lived on earth at the time. Can you imagine walking with Enoch and thinking about what it would be like for him when he walked into a city and encountered one of these giants or half-breeds and had to work around these animals that are hybrids? The dinosaurs were possibly there as well. That would be a bizarre world to live in. There would have to be a certain personality trait about Enoch that would cause him to be able to function. It would be much worse than it is today for us and much worse than it would be in the book of Acts.

- **Proverbs 28:1 ESV:**
  The wicked flee when no one pursues, but the righteous are bold as a lion.

  - There's fear involved with the wicked.
  - I've noticed that wealthy people are afraid of not having money. It's the craziest thing.
  - They're the stingiest people I have ever seen.
  - Not every rich person is stingy.
  - I've seen people that don't have money give. They're not afraid to offer everything.
  - I saw that there is self-preservation in certain wealthy people, and those that get to a certain status are afraid of losing that status.
  - It's fear-based.

❖ In this verse, Solomon talks about a good way to deal with the lack of boldness in your life.

- You can't have fear because fear has to do with torment.
- You have to be perfected in love and drive out fear.
- There are the wicked, and they are fleeing from someone who doesn't exist, according to how it's spoken here.
- They are not being pursued, but they're fleeing. The wicked do that because they're always afraid.
- The righteous are as bold as a lion.
- That means there was no fear in them based on the contrast of what's being discussed here.
- To me, boldness is a lack of fear.
- What is it that you need in your life? Do you need boldness, or do you just need to deal with fear?

❖ As believers, the Spirit of God gives us boldness. I believe we are as bold as a lion, but because of our personality, and this world, we have been conditioned to be a certain way.

- It's fear-based. We often don't know that the way we're responding and acting is because of fear.
- Once we deal with fear, what was given to us in Christ begins to work freely in our lives.

- Enoch was fearless. His calling, knowledge, and revelation caused him to walk on the earth boldly, knowing that God was with him.
- Even though he was pursued, and the creatures, hybrids, and giants wanted to kill him, he kept walking with God and was untouched.
- It knocked any rough edges off of him and sharpened his personality to the point that he was like God in many ways.
- Because of the hardship he went through, he became sure of himself.
- Once you get to that point, God preserves you
- He has favor over you; then you become confident in that, and that causes you to be bold.
- A very important aspect of Enoch was boldness.

**According to Proverbs 28:1, what is the trait of the wicked when they're not being pursued? How do the righteous respond?**

_____
_____
_____
_____

**How does fear hold us back? How do we overcome this using Enoch as an example?**

_____
_____
_____
_____

- ❖ **Acts 28:31 ESV:**

Proclaiming the kingdom of God and teaching about the Lord Jesus Christ with all boldness and without hindrance.

- Here's a verse that enforces all of those in the book of Acts who were proclaiming and teaching the kingdom, and they were talking about the Lord, but they were doing it with boldness, without fear, and without hindrance.
- They weren't hindered, but we've hindered ourselves through a hesitancy that we have, caused by fear.

## BOLDNESS IN OUR FAITH

- ❖ **Ephesians 3:12 ESV:**

In whom we have boldness and access with confidence through our faith in him.

- How we get boldness and access with confidence is through our faith in Him. Faith is the word trust.
- As you develop trust, then you gain confidence.
- That confidence causes you to have that boldness outwardly.
- When you pursue something, you must know it's yours, and if it's yours, then there is no denying you and no hesitancy.

- Boldness and access come with the confidence that you have through your faith in Him. The question is, do you trust Him? Trusting in Him gives you the confidence to take hold of that.
- That's what Enoch did. Enoch knew that he had an assignment.
- The book of Enoch reveals that he had three visions, one before the flood, one after the flood, and one at the end of days when he saw Jesus return.
- That's why Jude and 2 Peter talk about that and quote the book of Enoch.
- Enoch was a prophet who saw the plan of God. He was spoken of in Genesis chapters 5 and 6, and he had a vision about Jesus coming back the second time.
- He was profound and bold because he knew his part.
- You have to know your part.
- You have to know that you are in this for the plan of God to be accomplished.
- You have to have boldness.
- You've gained access, and you can have confidence.
- It's through your faith and trust in Him that it happens.
- You must develop your relationship with God and not worry about other people.
- Develop your own relationship with God and become a giver.
- When you encourage people and give of yourself to others, God will take care of you. That's how you flip it and gain access to God.

**How do you gain boldness?**

_____
_____
_____
_____


**How can you glean from what Enoch did? List some characteristics and ways he persevered.**

_____
_____
_____
_____


## BOLDNESS IN THE UPPER ROOM

- **Acts 4:31 ESV:**

  When they had prayed, the place in which they were gathered together was shaken, and they were all filled with the Holy Spirit and continued to speak the word of God with boldness.

  - They got together and prayed, and the whole place was shaken.
  - They were filled with the Holy Spirit, but this caused a boldness to come upon them, and they spoke the Word of God with that boldness.
  - That's what's going to happen to you.
  - It's already beginning to happen. It's happening with some of the adults but mostly with the children.

- I'm seeing boldness come upon them, and they're beginning to speak the Word of God. Especially the children.

❖ In the end time, it will appear that everyone is prophesying. It will appear that everyone is a prophet, and they will speak forth the will of God.

- Even if it's not happening, God still wants you to proclaim it.
- That's what Enoch did. He went around proclaiming the truth and speaking God's will, even if the people would not adhere to it.
- They were all going to be destroyed in the flood.
- The Spirit was prophesied.
- That's what I see happening in the days we're in.
- It's going to happen again, just like it was in the days of Noah.
- It's going to happen in our day too. It's already here.
- So the Holy Spirit came upon them, and they were filled.
- The result of the infilling of the Spirit was that they *continued* to preach the word of God and speak the word of God with boldness.
- They were as bold as a lion.

**How does unity in the Spirit with other believers create boldness?**

_____
_____
_____
_____

- **Acts 4:29 ESV:**

    And now, Lord, look upon their threats and grant to your servants to continue to speak your word with all boldness.

    - The prayer that they prayed was that they would have boldness.
    - We should be confident of God's message because we're confident of God. We should be confident that He is who He is and that anything He says, we're going to repeat it.
    - We'll speak what He's saying and do it with boldness because the spirit of boldness is what the early church prayed for.
    - I believe that Enoch was able to implement that into his life.
    - Even though he was set so far back in time, Enoch could grasp the personality of the Spirit of God and let that come through him.
    - It was probably overwhelming.
    - It was probably like what Samson experienced regarding all the things he did physically.
    - I believe that it was powerful for Enoch and these prophets as well.
    - The power of God was so strong that they couldn't shut up.
    - They had to say what they were supposed to say.

- **I see this happening in the end days. The same power that caused him to walk on the earth is the same power we have through Jesus Christ.**

- **The church will rise up and do these exploits in the coming days.**

**Where does boldness come from?**

_____
_____
_____
_____

## FEAR NOT FOR HE IS WITH YOU

❖ <u>**Hebrews 13:6 ESV:**</u>

So we can confidently say, "The Lord is my helper; I will not fear; what can man do to me?"

- That sums up everything about boldness.
- When you think about boldness, you think about being confident and saying, "the Lord is my helper."
- That is exactly what Enoch did.
- He relied on God to take care of him, and he didn't fear.
- It says here, "I will not fear. What can man do to me?"
- I'm sure Enoch quoted that all the time.
- Before he passed on to the other realm, he was probably saying at every step, "What can man do to me? If the Lord is with me, what can man do to me? The Lord is my helper."
- We should always rely on Him.

**What did Enoch do, and how can we, by example, walk with God?**

_____
_____
_____
_____

### KEEPING IN HOPE

❖ <u>**2 Corinthians 3:12 ESV:**</u>

Since we have such a hope, we are very bold.

- We see the discrepancies in our lives and the world we live in.
- Many things need to change, but you have to rely on hope.
- When you pray, it doesn't appear that things are changing, and that's because the body of Christ has to unite to destroy the demonic spirits that are controlling governments.
- It's not going to change by one person.
- We have emphasized certain individuals, and that's not what's in the word of God.
- We're supposed to be one body, and we're to be building each other up.
- That's how we take out the powerful, highly placed spirits over governments that control people in leadership and get into churches and infiltrate ministries.

- ❖ As the body of Christ, we need to break the power over ministers that are being controlled by these evil spirits they have handed themselves over to.

  - We need to have boldness. But sometimes, we just have to have hope.
  - That's what Paul was saying to the Corinthians, "since we have such a hope, we are very bold."
  - We are very bold, with hope.
  - If you back off because you feel like you don't have enough faith, remember the hope that you have and the hope of your calling.
  - There's a plan and a purpose for you, and you don't see everything that's happening.
  - Remain in hope and rely on the Spirit to take you into faith.
  - You can be very bold in hope alone.
  - Enoch had to be just like us. He had doubt and fear. I'm sure he had to go back to hope that God was working in his situation.
  - Many people are in similar situations, and God is saying to hold on; boldness will come even in hope.

**How does boldness relate to having hope?**

_____
_____
_____
_____

## OUR BOLDNESS COMES FROM JESUS

- **Acts 4:13 ESV:**

Now when they saw the boldness of Peter and John, and perceived that they were uneducated, common men, they were astonished. And they recognized that they had been with Jesus.

- People could see the boldness of Peter and John.
- I've noticed that people take advantage of you when you're unsure and not confident.
- When you are confident, people can sense it and don't want to mess with that.
- It was not easy to confront Jesus because He was very bold.
- I'm sure Enoch was set in his ways and confident in his beliefs.

**How can our confidence and hope in the Lord cause us to be bold?**

_____
_____
_____
_____

- I didn't get to talk to Enoch when I saw Him, but I was given a glimpse of what he was doing on earth. I saw him walking. It was a very short glimpse, but I could tell by how he handled himself that he was bold.

  - People in the New Testament church saw Peter and John as bold.

- They perceived or discerned that they were uneducated.
- They had to be thinking, if somebody is not educated, how could they be this bold?
- It doesn't add up because they were just common men.
- God is using all of us because we are just considered common. And those are the people that God uses.
- He doesn't use people that have all the abilities. He uses people that are willing.
- The common and uneducated end up being used by God more.
- This astonished people because it revealed that it had to be God; there was no way they could be that bold.
- They recognized that they had been with Jesus and associated that Jesus probably gave Him that boldness because of His boldness.

❖ It was the same as in the days of Noah when Noah and Enoch preached.

- We think about all those men walking in a time that was difficult.
- All the hybrids saw Enoch's boldness, but he probably wasn't known as being educated. He was a common man.
- He literally had animal skins on when I saw him, and he reminded me of a prophet or a John the Baptist type of person.
- In the coming days, I believe that people will be intimidated when they see the church and believers walking like in the days of Noah and walking as Enoch did in that boldness.
- They will know that it has to be God because there's no way anyone could be like that. It will make sense to them.

**God can use uneducated, common people to do great exploits and miracles. By our cultural standard, how is that opposite to the way we identify a successful or unsuccessful person?**

_____
_____
_____
_____

## HE IS WITH YOU AND IN YOUR MIDST

❖ <u>**Joshua 1:9 ESV:**</u>

"Have I not commanded you? Be strong and courageous. Do not be frightened, and do not be dismayed, for the Lord your God is with you wherever you go."

- Joshua had been commanded by the Lord. "Have I not commanded you?"
- That's different from a request.
- Joshua is receiving this word from the Lord, and he's being told, "I've commanded you to be strong. I've commanded you to be courageous."
- It all has to do with boldness.
- I saw that with Enoch and all the Old Testament prophets.
- They were bold because the Lord had commanded them.
- The word of the Lord had come to them, and it wasn't a suggestion.
- They were being told to do it.

- Jeremiah argued that he was too young, not influential, and didn't have boldness (Jeremiah 1:6-7).
- He decided to shut up and not prophesy anymore, but it began to burn within him, even into his bones (Jeremiah 20:9).
- Jeremiah said he couldn't help but prophesy and had to open his mouth.

❖ In the last days, I see people burning with fire and the word of the Lord, and they're going to prophesy.

- That was how I saw Enoch.
- It says, "Do not be frightened." So do not be in fear.
- When it says, "do not be dismayed," it means not being bewildered or puzzled over what you see.
- Be in love, not fear, "for the Lord your God is with you wherever you go."
- If God was with Joshua in the Old Testament, you know He is with you now. Wherever you go, He is with you.
- Get convinced of this because it will cause a boldness to come when you know that God is with you wherever you go.
- You have to reach a point where you know God is with you and that you're not going to do anything on your own.
- You want to do whatever the Lord has asked of you to do.
- You must become fully convinced and bold about it and know that God commands you to be strong and courageous.

**What are we commanded to do in Joshua 1:9?**

_____
_____
_____
_____

**How do God's commands give us boldness when we obey them?**

_____
_____
_____
_____

## CONFIDENT HOPE IN THE LORD

- ❖ **Ephesians 6:19 ESV:**

    And also for me, that words may be given to me in opening my mouth boldly to proclaim the mystery of the gospel.

    - Paul, the apostle, is asking that he would have boldness according to his ministry gift.
    - He was asking that he'd be able to speak the word of God openly and speak those words out boldly.
    - He asked God that he might boldly open his mouth and speak and that the words were given to him to proclaim the mystery of the gospel.

- We think of Paul as being the amazing person he is, yet he is asking God for help.
- He says, "And also for me, the words may be given to me in opening my mouth boldly to proclaim the mystery of the gospel."
- Paul asked for the mystery of the gospel that was solved when his eyes were opened, and he was taken to be with the Lord and taught all these things. Even he was requesting this.

**How, when we open our mouths, can we operate in boldness?**
_____
_____
_____
_____

❖ **Hebrews 4:16 ESV:**

Let us then with confidence draw near to the throne of grace, that we may receive mercy and find grace to help in time of need.

- We are not to crawl to the throne of grace sheepishly.
- We are supposed to walk in there boldly.
- We are to draw near with *confidence*, knowing that we have been requested to be in the presence of God.
- God has asked us to appear before Him, and we're drawn into His throne room of grace, which means it's unmerited favor.
- It means you can go in there; you are invited in.
- It's an open door, but it's not on your own merit.

- It's not because of your behavior.
- When you go in there, it's the throne of grace, which means God will do it for you because He loves you, not because He requires any more of you.
- He just wants you to show up. I know this to be the truth.

❖ If we show up to the throne of grace, which is that unmerited favor, we will receive mercy and find help in times of need. We can find this at the throne; it's not based on behavior.

- It's based on the fact that God has already provided it to us by grace. We have obtained this access.
- That's what Enoch did when I read his writings. He was translated. He was caught up. He was with the angels; he was with the Lord.
- He received counsel from the Lord and was shown the inner workings of the kingdom of God.
- It's an amazing story, but how much more for the Church, in this time that we live, should we have access and not only be invited in but won't want to leave.
- God doesn't have to command you to come to Him or request you to come to Him. You want to stay there, and you never want to leave.
- We have the confidence to draw near to the throne of grace.

**How do we access the throne of grace, and by whom? What do we receive at the throne?**

_____
_____
_____
_____

## THE GIFT OF GOD

- ❖ **2 Timothy 1:6-7 ESV:**

    For this reason I remind you to fan into flame the gift of God, which is in you through the laying on of my hands. For God gave us a spirit not of fear, but of power and love and self-control.

    - There are three different characteristics that the Spirit of God gives us; power, love, and self-control.
    - It says that God didn't give us a spirit of fear.
    - If we don't have fear, then we have boldness.
    - If you take away fear out of the equation, all that's left within you is boldness.
    - We are living the way we're supposed to when we have no fear.

- ❖ **Psalm 138:3 ESV:**

    On the day I called, you answered me; my strength of soul you increased.

- When the Psalmist prayed and called out to God, He answered, and that caused strength to come into his soul. He increased in his soul.
- That's not a spiritual thing necessarily. It's a psychological thing because the word for soul is different than the word for *spirit*.
- When God is faithful to you, answers you, and responds to you, it affects your soul and emotions.
- Take this to heart; sometimes, the relationship you have with God will take you further and faster than trying to do things to impress God to gain a position with God. Friendship with God is beyond that.
- God has called us friends now through Jesus Christ.
- Remember, God is going to answer you, and this will give you the boldness that you need.
- That's what happened with Enoch. It got to the place where his writings showed that God interacted with him.
- Enoch was way ahead of his time.
- It was as though he was in the New Testament with God.
- He had more interaction and boldness than most of us do in the New Testament church.
- It shouldn't be the way it is. We can learn from Enoch.

## PRAYER

Thank you, Lord, for everyone reading this and all the believers everywhere. Lord, that You would give them this boldness and that they would be able to do exploits for You. In the name of Jesus. Amen.

# CHAPTER TEN

# Tenacity is in You

*In all labor there is profit,*
*But mere talk leads only to poverty.*
—*Proverbs 14:23 AMP*

**DISCUSSION:**

It's not easy to live in this broken world. I can only imagine what it's like for you in your life. I only know what it is like for me and what I saw on the other side. I want to share the insight the Lord gave me and taught me when I was with Him. As we get closer to the end and begin to see things fade away, we need someone to mention certain words and aspects of the gospel that might not be preached. One of these words is tenacity, which I feel is being left out.

Tenacity has to do with endurance. When you think about long-distance runners being disciplined in a sport or profession, one characteristic they have is endurance. Many of you, who have a passion for something, know that if you want it, it will cost you. It's usually in the form of time and money. It will cost you a lot to get to where you need to go, especially if you've chosen a goal, whether it be education or a profession. When you pick up a musical instrument, you must practice and familiarize yourself with it. You have to practice repetition to master it. As a long-distance runner, you have to persevere to stay in there. When I ran, I had to stay in there even when it was getting painful or uncomfortable. When discomfort came in and you felt out of breath, you had to push to get better. It's not always fun to practice.

Tenacity is a trait that I believe Enoch had because he had to have endurance and stay in there to walk in a world full of hybrid people and animals and all the junk that was happening spiritually in those days. God said He would wipe out all of mankind and animals (Genesis 6:7). That's when you realize how bad it was.

Jesus, in the New Testament, appeared to John on the island of Patmos and said, "So then, because you are lukewarm, and neither cold nor hot, I will vomit you out of My mouth" (Revelation 3:16). Most churches are lukewarm, and so are Christians; they are lukewarm. I used to be that way too. I used to be casual about everything, even though I've had certain things happen to me. When I went to Heaven with Jesus, I saw how hot we need to be down here. I saw how the demonic works, and that's when my eyes were opened.

Enoch had to set himself in agreement with God and live each day walking with endurance staying in there. No matter what happens, whether good or bad, you must stay in there with the Lord. When things are going well, we tend to relax and not be diligent. I noticed with human behavior that when you achieve your near or long-term goal, you get excited and want to celebrate. But I've learned that after you accomplish a near-term goal, don't waste too much time celebrating over it. Make sure you go toward the next thing. That requires you to be tenacious and diligent.

Imagine Enoch having to deal with hybrid people and animals that were strange looking and acting. We see artwork that shows hybrid activity taking place. They weren't part of God's original creation. God wouldn't make a creature named the terrible lizard. That's what dinosaur means: terrible lizard. We know this based on the skeletons we found with them. We still have these types of vicious animals alive today, and we stay away from predators like that. There may have been dinosaur-like creatures roaming the earth with deformed and mutated hybrid people. Some hybrids were large and had abilities and powers. There must have been manipulation and witchcraft operating where they used their power to control people's minds.

As Christians, we want to be intentional in our lives, including developing personality traits to push us forward in our plan and purpose with God. Having tenacity means you are like a bulldog. You know when something is yours and when you are supposed to go, and you are passionate about aiming at your goal. The Lord showed me to bite down on it as a dog would. A bulldog would clamp down and not let go. The Lord just showed me this was tenaciousness and to grab on and never let go. He taught me to ride it out and never give up.

- ❖ **<u>Ephesians 1:11 ESV:</u>**
  In him we have obtained an inheritance, having been predestined according to the purpose of him who works all things according to the counsel of his will.

  - The prophets of the Old Testament and men and women of God in the New Testament church have to know what has been given to them.

- Tenacity causes you to have that. It's being aware that something has been given to you, and it's yours.
- What happened in the garden with Adam and Eve was that the serpent caused confusion, so they began to feel like they were left out.
- The serpent convinced them that they could have the fruit from that tree, which would make them wise. They already were wise.
- They didn't need to know evil; they only needed to know good.
- When they ate of the tree of the knowledge of good and evil, they could see both good and evil.
- It diminished them because they couldn't handle knowing evil.
- God never wanted us to know evil. It's good to know what is yours.
- If Eve had known what was hers, she would never have talked to the serpent
- The deception came in and caused a separation.
- That's what happens to most Christians.
- On the other side, I saw that we're separated from what we already have, so we are not fully convinced.
- As a result of that, we can't be tenacious or seem to function when we're not sure.
- We have to get rid of that hesitancy.

❖ The solution is to concentrate on what you know is yours. Paul talks about who we are in Christ and what has been given to us.

- He says we have obtained an inheritance.

- If you have something promised to you, like an inheritance, and it is distributed well, you have it in hand.
- It's been handed down or transferred to you, and it's yours now.
- There could be an instance when it's been promised to you, but the person hasn't given it to you, but it has been promised.
- You have the hope of that inheritance. It's essentially already been given to you; it's in your name. God planned it ahead of time.
- It's been a long time coming. It was before you were even born.
- It had your name on it, and now it's yours; it's been distributed.
- That's where I see Christians failing; they are hesitating because they don't know and aren't sure about what's theirs.
- You have to be sure and know that it's according to God's counsel and was determined ahead of time.
- God works everything out for His purpose.
- He's working it all out for His purpose in your life.
- You've been adopted in and given this inheritance, so it's yours.
- I wouldn't hesitate any longer.

❖ Meditate on Ephesians 1:11, and become sure so that you can clamp down like a bulldog and never let go.

- Expect your inheritance to appear and be distributed to be used in your lifetime.
- Every day you have provision based on this inheritance given to you long before you were born.

- That's your source. Your source is not people, your job, or anything else except God Himself. It was already determined and distributed before you were born.
- God is working everything out according to His purpose in the counsel of His will.
- Whatever He desires, He wants that for you, and that's what you ultimately want.
- Have the tenacity about you to say, "I am going to see this inheritance distributed and manifest."

**What is our inheritance in Christ, according to Ephesians 1:11?**

_____
_____
_____
_____

**What and who is your source?**

_____
_____
_____
_____

## WORTHY OF THE CALLING

- ❖ **<u>Ephesians 4:1 ESV:</u>**

  I therefore, a prisoner for the Lord, urge you to walk in a manner worthy of the calling to which you have been called.

  - Paul is encouraging people to walk in this inheritance, which is also a calling.
  - It requires action, but you use that inheritance while on earth to be faithful and do what God has called you to do.
  - We have been captured and are a prisoner for the Lord.
  - Your life is not your own. Your body is not your own, and your will is interwoven with God's will in your heart.
  - Paul is saying that because you are a prisoner of the Lord, you have been captured by the Lord and that you should walk in a manner worthy of the calling to which you have been called.

- ❖ Enoch walked in that calling as a prophet. He went around preaching and walking with God in a worthy manner, which means he was separate.

  - Enoch was on that highway of holiness that Isaiah talks about (Isaiah 35:8).
  - He walked separately, and he was captured and owned by the Lord.

- He got so caught up with the Lord that he could do amazing things and travel and preach and not let the war happening on earth physically get into him, which God was about ready to destroy.
- He allowed himself to be inserted into the war, but he didn't allow the war to get inside of him. He clamped down on his calling.
- The Scripture talks about the tenacity to clamp down not only on your inheritance but on your calling, and the calling causes you to walk worthily.
- You are going to walk in your calling and have an action about you, and people will see that.
- The angels are here to help you, and God will establish you on the earth and cause you to do exploits for Him.

**What is considered walking in a manner worthy of your call?**

_____
_____
_____
_____

## WALKING BY THE SPIRIT

❖ **1 Corinthians 2:14 ESV:**

The natural person does not accept the things of the Spirit of God, for they are folly to him, and he is not able to understand them because they are spiritually discerned

- To walk with God, Enoch had to walk in the Spirit.
- He didn't get caught up in what was happening in the physical down here on Earth. It caused him not to be hindered in the flesh.
- The person who walks with God pleases Him because he's listening to the impulses, suggestions, and commands of the Holy Spirit.
- The Spirit is nudging us all the time, but we might not be able to hear or sense His leading; however, we should.
- It means that we are spiritually dull if we don't.
- We need to focus and give more to our spiritual life and sow into it.
- The natural person doesn't accept the things of the Spirit because to do so requires a certain mindset.
- It's not you just being spiritual.

❖ A spiritual person can use their mind but agree with the Spirit and discern what's of the spirit, the flesh, and the mind.

- It has to do with agreeing with the Spirit but then being able to go with the Spirit in every situation.
- There are times when things will pull on you to go in a certain direction, and you have to be willing and able to know the natural response.
- I have watched Christians who should be well into walking in the Spirit because of their age or because they've walked with the Lord for a long time and don't respond correctly.
- It's not good for a person to sow into the flesh and to live by the flesh.

- You cannot produce anything of the Spirit or spiritual fruit from that. You have to be able to go with the Spirit.
- A spiritual person can follow the Lord in any situation, clamp down on that, and be discerning and tenacious.
- You must discern what the Spirit is saying, be tenacious enough to stay in there, and be disciplined to go with the Spirit, even if it makes you feel uncomfortable.

❖ I have learned that people don't want to say they're sorry and don't want to repent. They do not want to admit they were wrong.

- They go in a certain direction and continue to get hardened because they don't repent.
- I know people that would never admit they were wrong, and it doesn't take them very far because if you're not going to be accountable, you're not going to change.
- You have to be accountable if you want to see your routing change and end up where you're supposed to go.
- You have to be willing to admit that you could be wrong if something's not right. The Lord will never be wrong.
- I noticed that people don't want to blame God because it's embarrassing to say that God did something He didn't do, so they blame other people. They blame their circumstances. They blame the devil.
- The devil will be blamed because he is the god of this world, and we will blame him for everything.

- We have to take responsibility for ourselves and be tenacious and spiritually discerning.
- You must develop your senses in the Spirit to reap tomorrow what you have sown from the good decisions you made today.

❖ **You can imagine what it was like for Enoch. He was most likely getting into arguments and confrontations regularly.**

❖ **He had to have been supernaturally protected to function in the scenarios he faced at that time.**

❖ **I believe he was being translated and transported in the Spirit to escape being killed and that he was supernaturally sustained.**

❖ **How you respond to people is important because you don't want to get pulled into their war.**

❖ **We can learn from the prophets and what they went through by seeing that it's better not to respond to someone who is argumentative.**

**How does one sow into their spiritual lives?**

_____
_____
_____
_____

## WISDOM IS: NOT BEING PROVOKED

- ❖ **<u>Proverbs 15:1 ESV:</u>**

  A soft answer turns away wrath, but a harsh word stirs up anger.

  - There is wisdom in walking away and not arguing.
  - Don't give people any ammunition; let them say what they have to say and move on.
  - There's no need to argue with them because you are just throwing gasoline on the fire, and it's not worth it.
  - They're looking for an escalation, and Jesus taught this to me while reading about the Pharisees and how they dealt with Him.
  - You can learn a lot by seeing how Jesus handled these situations.
  - At times He provoked them to anger, but there were other times where He would ask them why they wanted to kill Him. Jesus would just ask them honestly.
  - He often responded with a soft answer or question.

- He didn't always respond to start a fight, although at times He did, because He was trying to expose them for who they were to the people in the crowds.
- "A soft answer turns away wrath."
- In these days that we live, we need to do that.

❖ Enoch learned to pick the battles the Lord wanted him to have, so he mostly proclaimed righteousness. He was a preacher of righteousness.

- He went around from city to city announcing the pending judgment because the Lord had told him that his son Methuselah would live until the flood came.
- The time of the flood would come when Methuselah died.
- Therefore, in the year that Methuselah died, the flood came because his name means *his death shall bring*, which brought the flood.
- We have to think as Enoch did.
- You don't need to win every argument. In fact, refrain from arguing.
- I told people I was sorry even when I didn't do anything wrong. I just didn't want to argue with certain people.
- You have to be that way, which will help you in the coming days.
- The Pharisees wanted to get Jesus into an argument, and he knew that.
- Sometimes He would not answer them, or He would ask them a question as the answer to the question they asked.
- It would block it to where they didn't want to go there, either.

- Another aspect of being tenacious is knowing when to talk and knowing when not to talk and realizing that you don't have to win every argument.

**How does Proverbs 15:1 teach us to handle harsh situations?**
_____
_____
_____
_____

## YOU MAY NOT BE RECEIVED

❖ **<u>John 1:11 ESV:</u>**

He came to his own, and his own people did not receive him.

- Here's another aspect of what Enoch most likely went through, and it's what Jesus went through.
- Jesus was rejected by the people that He was sent to help.
- Rejection is a big thing. We all have to overcome rejection and get to a place where if we're sent, we clamp down on that calling.
- We are tenacious, knowing that we are sent and doing it for God.
- The Gospel message has to be preached.
- If people reject it, they're not rejecting you; they're rejecting God.
- Jesus had to fulfill what His Father sent Him to do. He had to preach the good news and was not received by the people He was sent to.
- Enoch had to go from city to city to teach, preach, and prophesy, knowing that the people wouldn't turn.

- It happened with Jonah too. Jonah gave them a deadline, and he knew in his heart they wouldn't turn. They were evil people, but then they did turn, and Jonah was angry about it.
- With Enoch, the hybrids were not redeemable.
- God, in His righteousness, still had to have Enoch go around and preach for many years so that he would have done everything he could have done in his power.

❖ **For us to walk with God in this life and walk the way Enoch did, we must get over rejection. We cannot allow it to touch us in our souls and in our personalities.**

❖ **We have to get to that place where we see God's purpose is propelling us forward. Regardless of the response, it's not our responsibility; it is God's intention through us being sent into the world to preach and live out the message of God.**

❖ **If people reject it, then that is part of it. I don't expect half the people in the world to accept the message.**

❖ **Jesus taught us through His parables that it would happen. He told us to be excited when people reject and exclude us because great is our reward in Heaven (Luke 6:22-23).**

**When speaking the Word of God, how does rejection compel you to go further in ministry, as Jesus did? Whom are they rejecting?**

_____
_____
_____
_____

## GIVING THANKS TO THE LORD

- ❖ **<u>Psalm 138:2 ESV:</u>**

    I bow down toward your holy temple and give thanks to your name for your steadfast love and your faithfulness, for you have exalted above all things your name and your word.

    - Here David is talking about worshiping at God's temple.
    - That's David's lifestyle, and we should also adopt that lifestyle.
    - It says to "give thanks to Your name," and then David says profound words that have to do with tenacity.
    - These are the character traits that Enoch had and that we should have as the church and as believers.
    - We should be thankful for His steadfast love and faithfulness.
    - "Steadfast" means that God is anchored and never going to change.
    - He's always going to love you. He's never going to change that.
    - He's going to be faithful to you.

- Even when you're faithless, He will be faithful (2 Timothy 2:13).
- Even when you don't love, He's going to love still.
- You have to clamp down on these things because you're in a broken world that will reject you.

❖ The demons controlling people do not want us to operate in steadfastness or faithfulness because they know that if you are perfected in love, there's nothing they can do about you.
  - They can't stop you if you're walking in love, are fully convinced, and you're biting down on this with tenacity. They can't stop you when you know of God's faithfulness and steadfast love.
  - The Lord is exalted above all things, and His name and Word are also part of that.
  - Jesus Christ has been exalted above all things, but the name of Jesus is the name above all names. Not only is He exalted, but His Word is also exalted.
  - We must be fully convinced that He can perform whatever He has said.
  - If Enoch was called for that generation and walked with God in that generation, then he shouldn't be diminished in any way.
  - He should continue in his walk with God, just like you do.

**How do David's words and worship of God reveal his tenacity?**

_____
_____
_____
_____

**What caused David to bow down to God?**

_____
_____
_____
_____

**How will you carry out the tenacity in your life and love for God?**

_____
_____
_____
_____

## PRAYER

Father, in the name of Jesus. I thank You for Your power, that everyone will feel the power of God right now, and that they will have tenacity, beyond description, in the name of Jesus. Amen.

# SALVATION PRAYER

*Lord God,*
*I confess that I am a sinner.*
*I confess that I need Your Son, Jesus.*
*Please forgive me in His name.*
*Lord Jesus, I believe You died for me and that You*
*are alive and listening to me now.*
*I now turn from my sins and welcome*
*You into my heart. Come and take control of my life.*
*Make me the kind of person You want me to be.*
*Now, fill me with Your Holy Spirit, who will show me how to live for You.*
*I acknowledge You before men as my Savior and my Lord.*
*In Jesus' name. Amen.*

If you prayed this prayer, please contact us at
info@kevinzadai.com for more information and material.

We welcome you to join our network at Warriornotes.tv
for access to exclusive programming

To enroll in our ministry school, go to:
Warriornotesschool.com

**Visit KevinZadai.com for additional ministry materials**

# About Dr. Kevin Zadai

Kevin Zadai, Th.D., was called to the ministry at the age of ten. He attended Central Bible College in Springfield, Missouri, where he received a Bachelor of Arts in theology. Later, he received training in missions at Rhema Bible College and a Th. D. at Primus University. Dr. Kevin L. Zadai is dedicated to training Christians to live and operate in two realms at once— the supernatural and the natural. At age 31, Kevin met Jesus, got a second chance at life, and received a revelation that he could not fail because it's all rigged in our favor! Kevin holds a commercial pilot license and is retired from Southwest Airlines after twenty-nine years as a flight attendant. Kevin is the founder and president of Warrior Notes School of Ministry. He and his lovely wife, Kathi, reside in New Orleans, Louisiana.

# ENROLL IN DAYS OF HEAVEN ON EARTH AND HEAVENLY VISITATION AT NO COST!

## FREE ENROLLMENT

**WARRIORNOTESSCHOOL.COM**

# EARN YOUR ASSOCIATE, BACHELOR, MASTER, OR DOCTORATE DEGREES WITH DR. KEVIN ZADAI!

## WARRIOR NOTES SCHOOL OF MINISTRY IS AN ACCREDITED BIBLE COLLEGE

# CHECK OUT THESE OTHER RECENT STUDY GUIDES BY DR. KEVIN ZADAI

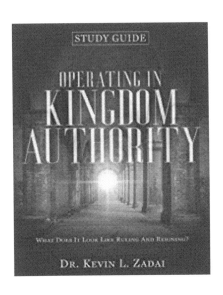 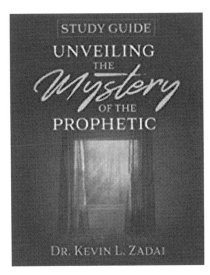 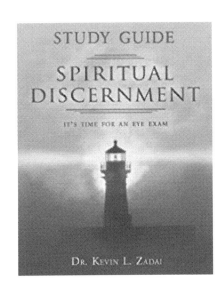

*Kevin has written over sixty books and study guides
Please see our website for a complete list of materials!
Kevinzadai.com*

Made in the USA
Middletown, DE
03 March 2023

26081575R00102